Towards Better Management of Secondary Education

A Report by the Audit Commission

May 1986

LONDON: HER MAJESTY'S STATIONERY OFFICE

ISBN 0 11 701294 7

# Table of Contents

# Glossary

| | |
|---|---|
| ALS | Activity-Led Staffing |
| AMMA | Assistant Masters and Mistresses Association |
| BTEC | Business and Technician Education Council |
| CDT | Craft, Design and Technology |
| CEO | Chief Education Officer |
| CGLI | City and Guilds of London Institute |
| CIPFA | Chartered Institute of Public Finance and Accountancy |
| CLEA/ST | Council of Local Education Authorities/School Teachers' Joint Committee |
| CLS | Curriculum-Led Staffing |
| CPVE | Certificate of Pre-Vocational Education |
| CSE | Certificate of Secondary Education |
| DES | Department of Education and Science |
| FE | Further Education |
| GCSE | General Certificate of Secondary Education |
| GRE | Grant Related Expenditure |
| HMI | Her Majesty's Inspectors of Schools |
| ILEA | Inner London Education Authority |
| LEA | Local Education Authority |
| MSC | Manpower Services Commission |
| NAHT | National Association of Head Teachers |
| NAS/UWT | National Association of Schoolmasters/Union of Women Teachers |
| NUT | National Union of Teachers |
| PAT | Professional Association of Teachers |
| PGCE | Post Graduate Certificate of Education |
| PE | Physical Education |
| PSBR | Public Sector Borrowing Requirement |
| PTR | Pupil Teacher Ratio |
| SHA | Secondary Heads Association |
| TRIST | TVEI Related In-Service Training |
| TVEI | Technical and Vocational Education Initiative |

# Summary

There are a disturbing number of indications that teaching costs – and teachers – are not being managed effectively. Costs per pupil have been increasing in real terms while there is a widespread public perception that swingeing cuts have been imposed. Although there is no general agreement on the appropriate secondary school curriculum or how it should be taught, the quality of secondary education is a continuing cause for concern: the proportion of school leavers with any A levels is still less than 20 per cent, almost exactly where it was over a decade ago; and over 40 per cent of school leavers still have no O levels at Grades A – C or their CSE equivalent. The proportion of students leaving at age 16 is very high by OECD standards; yet in the more deprived areas especially, absence levels of 25 per cent or more are not uncommon in some classes. Sickness absence amongst teachers – a barometer of staff morale – often exceeds 10 per cent on a typical school day. Teachers rarely receive any formal feedback on their performance. And there has been a failure to reward talented teachers properly; and there has been a notable increase in the number of younger teachers leaving the profession to take up other employment. Partly as a result, there are shortages of teachers for mathematics, physics and technology-based subjects in particular, and it is proving difficult to fill many head teacher posts. Small wonder, perhaps, that there has been sporadic industrial disruption for over 12 months.

Clearly, things cannot go on as they are.

Unfortunately, the prospects are for a bad situation to worsen. Local education authorities (LEAs) are in general not reorganising their schools to bring capacity into line with school rolls. As a result, money that should be spent on teaching is being devoted to maintaining, heating and cleaning redundant buildings and to teaching 'empty desks'. And the quality of education is bound to suffer as the curriculum will inevitably be curtailed to what can be afforded. A difficult problem will become more acute as secondary school rolls fall by a further 15 – 20 per cent over the next five years. Even if LEAs' present plans are implemented, the equivalent of over 1,000 secondary schools are likely to be standing completely empty within five years.

Recognising that the present situation is far from satisfactory, government plans fundamental changes to the examination system and the governance of secondary schools. And more radical possibilities are under discussion.

The Commission has no standing to comment on issues of education policy. Its concern and the focus of this report is management. The improvements necessary to secondary education in England and Wales are certain to cost money; and falling school rolls present an important opportunity to redirect investment over the next three to five years that will not come again. The scale of the resources potentially available is very considerable: £500 – 700 million a year by the end of the decade, or £2,500 – 4,000 per teacher. But major changes will be necessary if the opportunity is to be taken:

(i)   New incentives are needed to encourage authorities to reorganise their secondary schools and to adjust capacity in line with demand. It is reasonably obvious what needs to be done: around 1,000 secondary schools – 10 in a typical local education authority – need to be closed over the next four years, more than twice the current rate of closures. But the political process locally and nationally renders progress difficult – if not near impossible at times. Virtually all the vested interests oppose change; too often, the interests of current and future pupils and ratepayers are subordinated to those of local politics, parents of current pupils and teachers. The balance is weighted excessively in favour of the status quo. Shifting the balance will require such moves as:

   – streamlining the required consultation procedures which were framed to deal with the problems of a different (and more benign) era, in particular requiring more than ten local electors to object before the Secretary of State 'calls in' reorganisation schemes;

   – eliminating what amounts to a tax on reorganisation; because of the way the grant distribution systems works, £1 million invested in reorganisation can cost local ratepayers as much as £3 million in some cases;

   – exempting receipts from the sale of school land and buildings from the controls limiting local authorities' capital spending. Capital expenditure of the order of £2 billion will be needed over the next four to five years if the potential school closures are to take place; this is more than four times the expenditure now planned by government. LEAs must be enabled and encouraged to help themselves, by disposing of under-utilised school buildings and property and recycling some (at least) receipts into capital improvements in the schools that remain;

   – providing more incentives for local communities to press ahead with reorganising local secondary provision, e.g. through a capital grant to cover reorganisation costs or at least some of them; and reducing the scope for those protesting against reorganisation schemes agreed by the local authority to impose what are in effect extra taxes on their fellow citizens without the latter's agreement.

(ii)  The way teachers are assigned to schools needs to be changed. Most LEAs use some variant of the pupil:teacher ratio (PTR) to decide how many teachers each school should have. In practice, there is a wide variation in PTR among authorities from 11.3:1 to 18.1:1 and from school to school within an LEA. More important, use of the PTR as a means of deriving appropriate teacher complements for schools holds the following risks:

   – the ratio concentrates attention on inputs; the PTR has been "improving" over the last five years while the quality of secondary education has continued to give concern;

   – more attention needs to be devoted by LEAs and governors to the curriculum being offered by individual schools; and staffing levels must be consistent with whatever curriculum has been agreed. At present, schools can be left to square the circle: maintaining their current curriculum with insufficient teaching resources. This amounts to an abdication of the LEAs' statutory responsibility for the local education service;

   – the substantial resource represented by teachers' out-of-class time needs to be controlled: in the Inner London Education

Authority's secondary schools, out-of-class time represents 31 per cent of the average teacher's timetable in 1985; in shire counties the average is 22 per cent.

Each school's teaching complement should be determined by reference to the curriculum and the out-of-class activities which teachers are required to undertake. This can be achieved through an approach referred to in the report as Activity-Led Staffing (ALS). In addition to providing a more sensible and explicable way of assigning staff to schools the ALS approach forces authorities to face the economic and educational consequences of their decisions on the size of local secondary schools. It does not entail any assumption that the authority should set staff complements more or less generously; and members will need to set clear planning guidelines before the process begins.

(iii) More effort needs to be devoted to assessing individual schools' performance in adding educational 'value' to their pupils and to ensuring that head teachers are in a position to manage their school effectively. Good school management is directly reflected in education performance. So the selection and motivation of head teachers are key. This will mean more rigorous selection procedures, greater investment in in-service management training, better planning and control systems and fuller use of information technology.

(iv) Maximum authority should be delegated to the local (i.e. school) level. And the revenue budget and teaching complement should reflect the school's agreed role. The head and governors should then have the widest possible discretion to manage the school within the agreed budget, subject to appropriate quality assurance checks by the authority and the conditions set out in (iii) above. These powers should include:

- allocation of school resources in line with LEA's curriculum policy;
- regular assessment of teachers in relation to a broad-based contract of service;
- decisions on local recognition for teaching merit; regular assessment of teachers is essential and in principle superior performance should be reflected in pay;
- decisions on local arrangements for supply cover for absence and lunchtime supervision;
- control over school heating, cleaning, maintenance and repair priorities and contracts.

(v) LEAs should take more active steps to manage the number and mix of teachers in line with the agreed curriculum for their local schools. This will entail:

- better manpower planning, to take advantage of natural wastage. Some 12,000 teachers leave the profession voluntarily every year; and some 2,500 will be reaching retirement age every year for the next five to six years;
- use of early retirement and voluntary severance on a properly costed basis;
- more positive use of redeployment schemes (apparently a harsher approach than at present, but having benefits to the teacher as well as the pupil in terms of teachers' morale);
- limiting the use of 'ring-fences', i.e. schemes which allow each LEA's current employees first offers of jobs in that LEA;
- more use of part-time teachers, particularly by the adoption of a

'stepping down' scheme for those approaching retirement;

- greater investment in in-service training, which needs to be improved in all LEAs and not just in those able to attract Department of Education and Science (DES) in-service training grants by effective 'grantsmanship'.

To encourage LEAs to take those difficult steps, DES should arrange to ignore payments designed to secure early retirement or voluntary resignation of teachers surplus to local needs when entitlement to rate support grant is calculated.

(vi) New arrangements for determining pay and conditions of service for teachers should be introduced. The Burnham system has outlived its usefulness and is itself a source of some of the present management problems, blurring accountability and distorting management structures and career progression within schools. Pay and conditions of service should be negotiated together; and there should be substantial local flexibility within the nationally agreed terms and conditions of service, in particular to determine the appropriate arrangements for recruiting teachers for shortage subjects, managing teacher absence, providing cover for lunchtime supervision and recognising superior teaching performance.

These proposals do not represent a solution searching for a problem. Falling school rolls provide a considerable opportunity to devote more resources to teaching and less to maintaining, cleaning and heating buildings. The Commission calculates that over £1,000 a year per secondary school teacher is available in savings on non-teaching costs alone if possible reorganisation takes place. Nor is this report calling for more central control over the management of secondary education. In this, as in other aspects of local government, the need is for clear national strategic direction (e.g. over the secondary curriculum, examinations, the governance of schools and the education/training of 16–19 year olds) combined with more scope for local initiative in the management of teachers and schools and less detailed intervention by Ministers in local affairs. It should be clear where responsibility, authority and public accountability for the quality of the local education service lies: at present, the responsibilities of Ministers, LEAs and governors are still not sufficiently distinguished. Partly as a result, the prospects for closing schools on the scale required – of perhaps one in five – are poor.

And without school closures, the consequences will be serious: some combination of a continued under-rewarding of teachers, more limited curricula and higher costs than necessary for tax- and ratepayers. In short the prospects are for lower economy, efficiency and effectiveness in education terms – unless the steps set out in this report are implemented, and soon.

# Introduction

1. The *Local Government Finance Act* of 1982 requires the auditors appointed by the Audit Commission for Local Authorities in England and Wales (the Commission) to satisfy themselves that authorities have made "proper arrangements to secure economy, efficiency and effectiveness in the use of resources". Since education accounts for almost exactly half of total local government annual revenue expenditure, the Commission has already carried out studies of a number of different topics relevant to the education service. In particular, reports have been published on further education, non-teaching costs in secondary schools, energy management, purchasing and vehicle fleet management. Together, these reports and the local value for money projects which followed them have examined some 40 per cent of total local authority expenditure on education; and value improvements worth some £240 – 340 million a year seem possible eventually, as Exhibit 1 shows.

Exhibit 1

**COVERAGE OF PREVIOUS AUDIT COMMISSION REPORTS ON EDUCATION**
**% Gross Annual Expenditure**

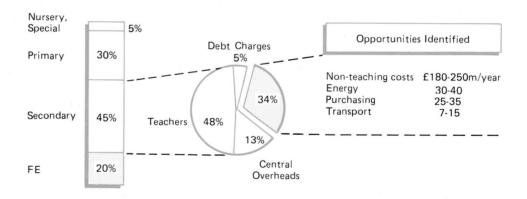

Source: Previous Audit Commission Reports

2. However, the Commission has not so far examined the management of the most important single resource in the nation's education service: school teachers. This report remedies the omission in respect of secondary schools. It deals with the way in which almost 240,000 secondary school teachers costing about £3 billion a year (in salaries and pension liabilities) are managed.

3. The team which carried out the Commission's study was led by Herbert Benham of the Commission's Special Studies Directorate. The team comprised three officers of the Special Studies Directorate, two deputy chief education officers seconded part-time for the period, a secondary school head teacher also seconded, and a lecturer from the Institute of Local Government Studies of the University of Birmingham. The study took place in the period November 1984 to October 1985. It drew on a wide range of material, notably from local education authorities and from DES. The main source of information, however, was 12 participating authorities which were all visited by members of the study team. Within these 12, a total of 74 schools was visited in addition to the education departments. The study authorities consisted of two outer London boroughs, three metropolitan districts and seven shire counties. They were chosen to give a variety of authority type, geographic location, size and socio-economic characteristics.

Questionnaires and aides-memoire were compiled to ensure that topics identified by the team as important were covered in investigations in each authority. The questionnaires and aide-memoires were used in interviews with education committee members, chief education officers and education department staff, head teachers and some of their staff, teacher association representatives and finance staff. And the team reviewed auditors' reports to 55 local education authorities (LEAs) on progress in tailoring secondary school capacity to likely demand. The conclusions arising from the work have been discussed with a wide cross-section of the interests involved. The Commission acknowledges with gratitude the help and co-operation afforded by the 12 participating authorities as well as the education committees in Essex, Leeds and Trafford for releasing senior personnel to work on this study. However, the conclusions here are the Commission's.

4. The Commission, like many other observers, is deeply disturbed at the situation. The Commission is not competent to make educational judgements; and it has avoided doing so in this report. But there are many indications that radical reform of the way teachers are managed is now overdue, quite apart from the prolonged industrial dispute. There are serious shortages of teachers in technical subjects such as mathematics and physics; it is proving difficult to fill vacancies for head teacher posts in many instances; costs per secondary school pupil have risen by some 18.5 per cent in real terms in the period 1979–85, but the educational benefits that might be expected to flow from additional expenditure of over £500 million a year are not immediately apparent to many observers.

5. All these symptoms would be a cause for management concern in any business. In the case of secondary education, the service faces four serious external challenges as well:

- Falling numbers. It is invariably easier to manage growth than to cope with the effects of lower demand for services, as many industrial concerns have found over the past decade. Secondary schools face a fall in the number of pupils of nearly 20 per cent over the next five years. In many authorities, many of them in hard-pressed urban areas, the fall would be much greater than this.
- Challenge to existing quality standards. The Commission is not competent to assess the quality of current secondary school education. But it observes serious and widespread concern. The titles of two recent White Papers, *Teaching Quality* and *Better Schools,* reflect government's view, which seems to be widely shared, that major improvements in standards are both necessary and possible.

– Demands that education should be relevant to employment and adult life. The philosophic divide between 'education' and 'training' runs very deep; but the validity of the traditional distinction and its relevance to our schools is now under increasing challenge. The growth of youth unemployment and Britain's poor economic performance have led to increased questioning of the relevance of the curriculum of schools. There is a desire to make the curriculum more relevant to pupils and the world they will experience after leaving school. Major changes are proposed in the nature of the curriculum and its content, particularly in the emphasis on technical and vocational education; and new examination systems and methods of assessment are being introduced. Significant changes and initiatives now appear frequently and their adoption implies added work for LEAs and schools, for example, the General Certificate of Secondary Education (GCSE), the Technical and Vocational Education Initiative (TVEI), TVEI Related In-Service Training, (TRIST), profiling, and many others. Moreover, these innovations frequently require working with outside agencies such as the Manpower Services Commission (MSC).

– Declining support from central government for local education services. It is not for the Commission to comment on government's expenditure plans and priorities. But analysis of the *Government's Expenditure Plans* for the period to 1988–89 shows that it expects to see no real increase in revenue expenditure per secondary school pupil; and the extent of government support to local authorities has declined steadily in real terms since the mid 1970s: in 1985–86 prices, the annual rate support grant has declined from £11,554m in 1979–80 to £8,753m in 1985–86.

6. The management of the education service is thus becoming more difficult as the constraints and demands change. More individuals and external bodies are becoming involved in the process. Schools are expected to develop closer links with the local community and with local industry and commerce. Education authorities must negotiate with central government and with MSC in order to develop their programmes. Exhibit 2 summarises

Exhibit 2

**THE MANAGEMENT CHALLENGE IN SECONDARY EDUCATION**

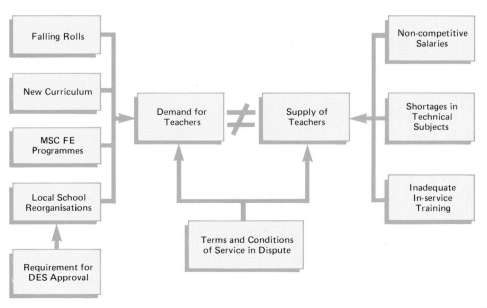

the nature of the management challenge which this report addresses. It is clearly a daunting one, not made any easier by the uncertainty generated by speculation about possible initiatives such as Crown schools and education vouchers or by the general lack of a managerial "ethos" within education: the professional journals provide frequent evidence that many educationalists consider management as little more than a threat to educational quality and a means of making cuts relatively painlessly. But in the Commission's view the very severity of the challenge holds promise for the future. It is clear that things cannot go on as they are: a policy of "more of the same, only better" will plainly not be adequate. Parliament, LEAs and the teachers themselves must surely be prepared for the difficult decisions – most notably over school closures – which seem likely to be necessary if the secondary education system is not to settle for a prolonged period of relative decline because of lack of resources.

7. Falling school rolls present a considerable opportunity to finance essential improvements over the next three to five years. Resources that are now invested in under-utilised land and buildings – and teachers – could be redeployed to improve teachers' relative pay and to provide the kind of buildings and equipment appropriate to the needs of the 21st century. The sums involved are very large: over £700 million a year at 1985 prices could be available by 1990, the equivalent of over £4,000 a year per teacher. But painful choices will have to be made soon, since the "window of opportunity" will begin to close in the early 1990s and five years have passed already. And at present the service is not well equipped to face such choices. So there is the uncomfortable prospect of continued muddle and "fudge" unless radical changes are made.

8. The report that follows is therefore in three parts, reflecting the Commission's three main conclusions:

(i)   *Local education authorities can manage their teaching resources better* despite the present legislative and other constraints. The local reorganisation of secondary schools needs to be accelerated, so that an appropriately broad curriculum can be maintained with the available resources; the basis on which teachers are assigned to schools needs to be changed, to reflect the curriculum rather than simply the number of pupils or past establishment levels; more responsibility and authority need to be delegated to the local level – and, as a corollary, more attention must be paid to the way head teachers are selected and trained; further steps need to be taken to ensure that all teachers are competent in the subjects for which they are responsible. Chapter One of this report describes the steps that the Commission considers can and should be taken immediately to improve the management of secondary education within the constraints of the existing system. These steps will be the focus of auditors' attention during the 1986–87 audit round.

(ii)  *More radical changes will be needed if the available opportunities are to be taken.* The Commission has concluded that without fundamental changes in the way the education service is managed, some involving legislation, the prospects for action along the lines suggested in Chapter One are unacceptably poor. The roles and responsibilities of the Secretary of State, LEAs and governing bodies are confused, and, as a result, the accountability for the quality for the local education service is blurred. DES officials are spending too much time "second guessing" local managers. In the meantime, important issues are not given adequate attention: serious flaws in the system for distributing grant and controlling capital spending have been perpetuated; the arrangements for negotiating pay and conditions of service for teachers are plainly inappropriate; the systems for securing agreement to local school reorganisations make a difficult problem worse. Chapter Two, therefore, identifies some of the key issues that will need to be addressed at the national level if the opportunity presented by falling school rolls is to be grasped.

(iii) *Time is short.* As stated above, the "window of opportunity" will begin to close in the early 1990s, as secondary school rolls stabilise and then begin to rise. And five years have already gone. So the final chapter of this report sets out the next steps for local authorities and central government.

9. As is often the case, other nations are facing similar problems. In April 1983, the report of the National Commission on Excellence in Education was published in the United States. It was entitled *A Nation at Risk: the Imperative for Educational Reform.*\* The report concluded (page 5) that "the educational foundations of our society are presently being eroded by a rising tide of mediocrity that threatens our very future as a Nation and a people. What was unimaginable a generation ago has begun to occur – others are matching and surpassing our educational attainments . . . our society and its educational institutions seems to have lost sight of the basic purposes of schooling and of the high expectations and discipline needed to attain them. . . this is hardly surprising given the multitude of often conflicting demands we have placed on our Nation's schools and colleges. They are routinely called on to provide solutions to personal, social and political problems that the home and other institutions will not or cannot resolve. We must understand that these demands. . . often exact educational cost as well as a financial one".

10. Nobody has suggested to the Commission that the situation in England and Wales is as serious – yet. But many observers say that it could become so all too easily unless the appropriate management action is taken over the next few years. The purpose of this report and of the local projects that will follow next year is to prevent further deterioration in the wake of the present industrial dispute, in the belief that the quality of secondary education can be improved within the existing resources. In short, this report is designed to secure better value for a very large element of the education service which itself accounts for over half of gross local government spending every year.

---

\*Available from the Superintendent of Documents, US Government Printing Office, Washington DC.

# 1 Managing Teaching Better Within Existing Constraints

11. Teachers are a precious resource. They determine the quality of secondary education and the way they are deployed determines its cost to a large extent. Like any scarce and expensive resource they must be managed, within the constraints of a professional ethos and of the present system – it is not generally particularly useful, in the near term at least, to argue that "we should not be starting from here". In the Commission's view, the sound management of teachers requires that:

(i)   Teaching resources are not wasted. Within the limits of appropriate group sizes for particular subjects, empty seats in any class represent a wasted opportunity for a teacher to impart knowledge and enthusiasm for a subject. As school rolls fall, the waste entailed by empty seats will become more serious unless schools are reorganised on a scale which has hitherto proved impossible.

(ii)  Teaching resources are allocated to schools in line with the LEA's stated curricular objectives.

(iii) LEAs ensure that school staffing levels match the agreed establishment.

(iv)  Head teachers have the authority, and the skills to go with it, to manage the resources allocated by the LEA; management by remote control is no more appropriate in the context of schools than it is in other spheres.

(v)   Sufficient resources are devoted to sustaining the quality of teachers, so that they are competent to teach the subjects and pupils for whom they are responsible.

The study suggests that these basic management requirements are not now being met in many authorities; and the rest of this chapter sets out the corrective action required.

**REORGANISING SCHOOLS TO REDUCE WASTE OF TEACHING SKILLS**

12. In its report published in December 1984, *Obtaining Better Value in Education: Aspects of Non-Teaching Costs in Secondary Schools*\*, the Commission drew attention to the fact that secondary school rolls were set to fall and suggested how LEAs should seek to tailor school capacity to likely demand. However, analysis of auditors' recent reports suggests that progress in reorganising schools has been slow and that the prospects for action on the scale required are, generally, poor. This is extremely regrettable for the following reasons:

(i)   A major opportunity will be lost: falling school rolls could mean that perhaps as much as £700 million a year (at present prices) could be available for redeployment by the early 1990s.

(ii)  But unless schools are closed, the possible benefits will not be fully realised; and many authorities are taking the "soft option" of removing surplus places without closing schools. This minimises local political problems; but it will lead either to higher costs or to a more limited curriculum and most likely to both.

---

\*ISBN 0 11 701092 8. HMSO Price £4.20 net.

(iii) Time is running out. The lead time necessary to implement any local reorganisation is up to five years; and the process will need to be completed by the early 1990s at the latest. But the majority of authorities appear not even to have formulated a strategic response to the fall in rolls.

Each of these reasons is discussed in detail below.

**A £700 million opportunity**

13. The number of secondary age school pupils is falling sharply. Exhibit 3 shows secondary pupil numbers from 1979 to 2000. From the peak in 1979 to the trough in 1991 the fall is from 4.1 million to 3.0 million, a drop of 27 per cent. In many areas, the fall is likely to be much greater than this. A reduction as dramatic as this provides the opportunity for freeing substantial teaching resources to reduce local authority expenditure, to increase provision for other local authority services or to implement educational innovations. If it were possible to maintain the secondary PTR at the level of 1979, the size of the saving from 1979 to 1991 would be 67,000 teachers, equivalent to £830 million per annum assuming the 1986 average cost per teacher; and non-teaching costs – heating, caretaking, cleaning and maintenance of buildings would save a further £150 – 200 million.

Exhibit 3

## NUMBERS OF SECONDARY SCHOOL PUPILS, 1979-2000
**England and Wales**

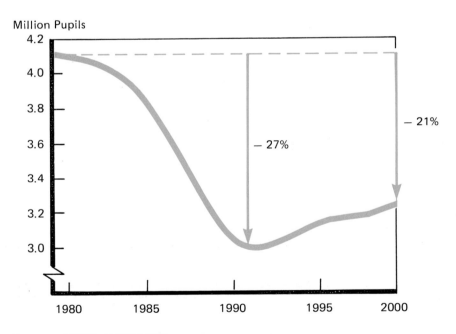

Million Pupils

Sources: CIPFA (1979-1986)
Advisory Committee [to the DES]
on the Supply and Education of Teachers (ACSET)

14. Of course, there are limits on the extent to which resources can be redeployed. The need to allow for parental choice, for the requirements of special education and for the eventual upturn in pupil numbers in the early 1990s means that it would be unwise to seek to remove all spare capacity; a "safety" margin will always be necessary. In any case, education authorities may judge, for example, that small schools cannot be closed where closure would inflict an unacceptably long journey to school on pupils.

15. One view of the extent to which teaching resources could be freed is that of the Working Group on Schoolteacher Numbers and Deployment in the Longer Term, a joint body of DES and the local authority associations. The Working Group assessed the effect of different rates of schools' reorganisation by assuming that each school's teacher complement was divided between "overhead" teachers (analogous to fixed costs) and other teachers, whose numbers are proportional to pupil numbers. Exhibit 4 shows projections of teacher numbers derived from those produced by the group, together with associated projections of the national secondary PTR. In both graphs, the upper and lower curves correspond to the extreme assumptions about the rate at which school capacity is brought into line with school populations. The top line corresponds to minimal reorganisation of schools whilst the bottom line shows projected teacher numbers if school closures maintain the present average school size. A general addition of 6.34 per cent to all the Group's figures (pro rata to the projected numbers of pupils) has been included to make allowance for Wales since there are no recent comparable projections for the Principality. These projections imply a reduction in teacher complements of between 48,000 and 55,000 teachers over the period 1984 to 1991 with no worsening or improvement in educational provision, corresponding to a cost reduction of between £590 million and £680 million per annum at 1986 cost levels. Given the make-up of the group, it is reasonable to presume that these are fairly conservative estimates of what could be achieved with sufficient local determination.

Exhibit 4

**REQUIREMENTS FOR MAINTAINING SECONDARY SCHOOL EDUCATION PROVISION UNDER DIFFERENT CLOSURE ASSUMPTIONS, 1984-1991**

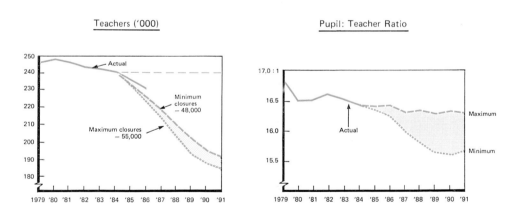

Source: Audit Commission Analysis of the Report of the Working Group on School Teacher Numbers and Deployment, September 1985 (except base case) CIPFA (actuals)

16. Savings from rationalising secondary school capacity will enable LEAs to respond more readily to educational initiatives from central government which will require extra teachers. Estimates, albeit tentative, have been made of the extra teacher requirements of some recent initiatives:

(a) For new examinations and for the keeping of records of pupils' achievements, the Group estimates that 2,000 teachers are needed.

(b) The Technical and Vocational Educational Initiative (TVEI) is aimed at increasing the vocational content of educational courses. In every LEA where TVEI is being implemented it has resulted in an increase in staffing. The overall national effect on the requirement for teachers will not be known until the extent of implementation has been decided. The Working Group referred to above has quoted a range of 5,000 – 7,000 new teachers as the addition needed for all currently proposed curricular innovations, including TVEI.

(c) Increased attention to the induction of teachers new to the profession and increased employment of occasional teachers to cover other teachers' absence are each seen as leading to the employment of between 500 and 600 teachers.

(d) Pupils with special needs are increasingly to be educated in ordinary schools following the 1981 *Education Act*. The estimate of the additional teacher requirement to designate in every school a teacher to "take responsibility for work with pupils with special needs" is half of one teacher's time per secondary school, which would amount to some 2,000 teachers in all.

In addition, as discussed below, extra investment of teaching time is likely to be required for the preparation of classes, increases in in-service training and for local management (including the assessment of individual teachers' performance).

17. More important, the funds wasted on teaching empty chairs and maintaining, heating and cleaning redundant classrooms will not be available to improve teachers' relative pay and to enhance the educational facilities; books and equipment as well as the curriculum available to pupils. Teaching costs account for 68 per cent of the total annual cost of secondary education of £1,139 per pupil. Since central grant support of the order of £450 – 600 per pupil (depending on the authority) is based on the number of pupils on school rolls, it follows that if no action is taken to reorganise local school systems, LEAs will face an uncomfortable choice between placing extra burdens on the local ratepayers, cutting the curriculum or "penny pinching" on maintenance, books and equipment.

18. Given the *minimum* closures shown in Exhibit 4, the potential resources available for redeployment in the early 1990s amount to some £450 million a year, the equivalent of almost £2,400 per teacher in 1990, or 20 per cent of current annual average salary levels. This saving can only be achieved at the cost of appreciable investment (notably in re-training of teachers and in adaptation of buildings) but on any reasonable estimates, the savings provide returns on this investment well in excess of 30 per cent. Table 1 provides the details of the savings compared with 1984 cost levels that could be available by 1991 (using estimates of teacher numbers from paragraphs 14 and 15 and on a range of projections of building capacity).

*Table 1:* POTENTIAL SAVINGS IN 1991, COMPARED WITH 1984
£ million, at 1986 prices

|  | Minimum | Maximum |
|---|---|---|
| Teaching costs | | |
| – falling rolls and school closures | £590 m | 680 |
| – new initiatives | (220) | (170) |
| Non-teaching costs | 80 | 200 |
| TOTAL | 450 | 710 |

However, this potential will only be fully realised if schools are closed and teaching and other resources concentrated in high-quality facilities that are large enough to sustain a broad-based curriculum appropriate to the needs of an internationally competitive economy in the 21st century. At present, LEAs are, generally, failing to grasp the opportunities that are available.

19. Authorities can respond in one of three ways to the opportunity that falling school rolls presents. At the extreme they could:

(a) Maintain the existing number of schools and teachers, and endeavour to maintain the current curriculum, inevitably at vastly increased unit costs; or

(b) Reduce the number of schools and teachers at a rate which maintains current curricula with reduced total expenditure and unit costs kept at current levels; or

(c) Maintain the existing number of schools but reduce the number of teachers in line with falling school rolls, at once impoverishing the curriculum and failing to take advantage of the cost savings which capacity rationalisation would bring.

20. The Commission favours the adoption of the second position as far as possible: the first is wasteful in terms of scarce teaching skills (since group sizes will be unduly small) and the costs of heating, cleaning and maintaining school buildings. And the third is an unnecessary worsening of provision. Sadly, the evidence suggests that many LEAs are adopting precisely the wrong, short-sighted, strategy of seeking to hang on to buildings at the expense of the quality of education:

− The reduction in the number of teachers to date, more than half way through the period of falling secondary school rolls, does not match even the slowest rate of run-down considered by the Working Group advising the Secretary of State. At present there are some 5,000 more teachers in post (costing some £65 million a year) than the number required to maintain education provision under *minimum* closure assumptions.

− Costs per pupil are rising; but much of the increased spending is not reflected in the quality of the education that each pupil receives. Exhibit 5 shows the source of the real increase of 18.6 per cent in costs per pupil since 1979. It indicates that under half

Exhibit 5

**SOURCE OF REAL INCREASE (ABOVE RPI) IN EDUCATION COSTS PER SECONDARY PUPIL 1979-1985**

**£ at September 30, 1985 prices**

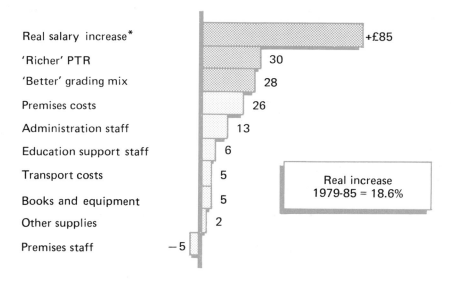

Real salary increase* +£85
'Richer' PTR 30
'Better' grading mix 28
Premises costs 26
Administration staff 13
Education support staff 6
Transport costs 5
Books and equipment 5
Other supplies 2
Premises staff −5

Real increase 1979-85 = 18.6%

\* Assumes 6% increase for 1985-86

Source: Audit Commission analysis of CIPFA Education Statistics, 1985-86 estimates

of the increase has been the result of improving teachers' relative pay and paying for more books and equipment (indeed, since the average cost of paper to educational book publishers increased faster than the retail price index during the period, the exhibit suggests that the number of books purchased fell by some 4 – 5 per cent during the period). And some 40 per cent of the increase has been attributable directly or otherwise to delays in reorganising local secondary schools as rolls have fallen.

- An increasing number of schools are too small to be educationally viable. Smaller schools are more expensive to staff if they are to deliver the same curriculum, especially as they fall below four forms of entry. There are also other problems with small schools. It may be difficult, for example, to allow children significant option choice without group sizes becoming uneconomically small. There are simply too few pupils to fit into an extensive option system. The distribution of the actual sizes of schools can be shown from published DES statistics. Her Majesty's Inspectors of Schools (HMI) consider that for comprehensive schools six forms of entry (implying a total roll of some 900 for a school taking pupils in at age 11 without a sixth form) are necessary to support the appropriate breadth of choice within the curriculum. Yet analysis of auditors' reports to LEAs suggests that approximately one quarter of schools now have *four or fewer* forms of entry and are thus definitely too small to be educationally viable, according to HMI. Table 2 below compares the sizes of comprehensive schools in England in January 1979 and 1985.

*Table 2:* SIZE DISTRIBUTION OF COMPREHENSIVE SCHOOLS
England

| School Roll in January | Number of Schools | | |
| --- | --- | --- | --- |
| | 1979 | 1985 | Change |
| ≤ 400 | 124 | 120 | (4) |
| 401 – 600 | 390 | 408 | 18 |
| 601 – 800 | 595 | 713 | 118 |
| 801 – 1,000 | 739 | 831 | 92 |
| 1,001 – 1,500 | 1,122 | 1,015 | (107) |
| > 1,500 | 233 | 162 | (71) |
| [Average Secondary roll | 941 | 878 | – 6.7%] |

The situation will deteriorate further over the next five years since rolls fell by eight per cent between 1979 and 1985 and are expected to fall by a further 19 per cent between 1985 and 1991.

- These trends are reflected in small group sizes in many schools. In January 1984, 23.5 per cent of classes mainly for 14 and 15 year olds had 15 or fewer pupils and 57.4 per cent of classes mainly for pupils 16 and over had 10 or fewer pupils. The position in the sixth forms is especially serious, particularly given the present shortage of teachers of mathematics, physics and craft, design and technology (CDT).

21. Reviews of auditors' reports to LEAs prepared in 1985 confirm the general picture emerging from the analysis. Only around one LEA in four has specific plans to reorganise local secondary school provision that have been agreed (where the law requires) by the Secretary of State for Education and Science. Almost two thirds have made no strategic response to the fall in rolls which has been under way for five years or more. Table 3 summarises the situation:

Table 3:  AUTHORITIES' MAIN RESPONSE TO DATE TO FALLING SCHOOL ROLLS
% Sample LEAs (n = 55)

| | |
|---|---|
| No strategic response being developed | 26% |
| Working party established | 20 |
| Avoid closures, remove temporary accommodation | 18 |
| Rationalisation plans under local discussion | 11 |
| Reorganisation agreed, implementation under way | 25 |

22. However, auditors' reports also indicate that some authorities have taken the difficult and often painful steps to close schools despite the political and management risks involved for all concerned. For example, among the authorities that have adopted a strategic response:

– Barnet has reduced capacity by 19 forms of entry (out of 128) since 1978, but still faces spare capacity of at least nine forms of entry; and most of its 21 schools are below the "viability" level of six forms of entry in autumn 1984.

| Forms of entry | Number of schools |
|---|---|
| < 4 | 4 |
| 4 – 5 | 5 |
| 5 – 6 | 9 |
| > 6 | 3 |
| | 21 |

– Bexley is planning to reduce its secondary schools to 88 forms of entry from the present 119 (a reduction of over 26 per cent) and will be taking over 3,300 places out of use and closing/amalgamating five schools out of 19. Even so, by 1991 there will be 25 per cent spare capacity unless further action is taken.

– Birmingham commenced a major reorganisation in September 1983 which is still being implemented. The reorganisation involves the closing of seven schools (out of a total of 97), the amalgamation of eight pairs of schools, the conversion of three schools in the 18–19 age group into sixth form colleges and the removal of 32 sixth forms. Even so, without further steps, by 1991 the spare capacity in the city's schools will have risen from 14 per cent now to 23 per cent.

– Dorset has agreed to remove 3,040 places by the end of 1988, out of a current capacity of around 35,000; even so, by 1991, there will be some 5,900 "spare" places in the county's schools.

– Gateshead has proposed a system of secondary schools for 11–16 year olds with a tertiary college for students aged 16+. Two schools (out of 17) will be closed; and a further two will become part of the new tertiary college. Even so, by 1990 there will be 2,780 surplus places, with two schools (both near the council borders) with a combined capacity of some 3,250 places having fewer than 1,500 students between them.

– Haringey has closed four out of 14 secondary schools since 1977, but still faces 25 per cent spare capacity within three to four years unless further steps are taken.

– Hertfordshire began its review of secondary school provision in 1978–79. Since then seven schools have been closed and eight amalgamations have been implemented, involving 6,750 places; a further 10 closures or amalgamations have been proposed which will mean 5,850 places being taken out of use. Twelve sites will be sold.

– Manchester has made plans to move 75 per cent of the maximum forecast surplus which will occur in September 1989; plans are also in hand to impose admission limits, reorganise the Roman Catholic voluntary schools and to reorganise sixth form provision. Fourteen major buildings (out of 37) are surplus to requirements and will be sold with an estimated site value (at 1980 values) of over £4 million. Altogether some 11,000 places will be taken out of use over the next three to four years.

– In 1983–84, Redbridge carried out a comprehensive review of its secondary school provision and concluded after exhaustive consultation with the interested parties and a full financial appraisal that the best way to remove surplus places was to close two schools, and to reduce the level of first form entry in eight schools. The latter proposal made it easier to amalgamate five split site schools, thus releasing the lower sites for alternative use or sale. Despite these measures which affected more than half of the borough's 16 secondary schools, there will remain some 1,500 (13 per cent) spare places in the early 1990s.

– Waltham Forest has adopted a comprehensive, open and staged approach with considerable public consultations. The reorganisation will commence in September 1986 and will involve taking 2,200 places a year out of use. Seven school buildings or sites will be sold in due course and the proceeds invested in the local education system.

However, these examples are the exception, not the rule; and even in these cases, the prospects are for spare capacity to increase from 15 per cent now to 20 per cent in 1991. Reviews of auditors' reports and of Chief Education Officers' (CEOs) responses to the Commission's recent questionnaire suggest that no change in the situation is imminent: only around one LEA in four is prepared for significant rationalisation of its secondary school capacity as rolls fall. As a result, in the early 1990s the equivalent of well over 1,000 secondary schools will be standing completely empty. The implications are extremely serious. Perhaps as much as £500 million a year of resources could be released and facilities will be wasted, "teaching" empty desks and maintaining, heating and cleaning redundant buildings.

**Need for urgent action**

23. There is little time to lose if the opportunities presented by falling rolls are to be taken in time. Secondary school rolls will begin to rise again in many areas in the early 1990s, providing an all too convenient excuse for those seeking to avoid painful closures. From the beginning of the planning effort to implementation of a reorganisation scheme can easily take four to five years – including the time necessary to secure the approval of the Secretary of State. So within the next two years at most, plans need to be drawn up and agreed to close perhaps as many as 1,000 schools by the end of 1990. As was stated above, analysis of auditors' reports suggests that the situation as at January 1986 was far from satisfactory. As Exhibit 6 shows, the prospect is for the spare capacity to increase sharply by the end of the decade. The Exhibit is based on the reports from a sample of 46 LEAs accounting for almost exactly half of secondary pupils in England and Wales in 1986. At the national level, it suggests that there will be an increase of at least 500,000 empty places between now and 1991 unless plans change. This projection is consistent with available information on the "pipeline" of reorganisation proposals. Rolls are projected to decline by some 700,000 between 1986 and 1991 but only around 150,000 places will be removed as a result of decisions already taken or in prospect. Removal of approximately 97,000 places is likely as a result of decisions on secondary school

reorganisations taken by the Secretary of State in 1984 and 1985; and Table 4 below shows the number of formal proposals outstanding at the end of January 1986 which, if all are accepted, might entail a further reduction of 40–50,000 places.

*Table 4:* "PIPELINE" OF SECONDARY SCHOOL CLOSURES
Proposals undecided by Secretary of State at January 31, 1986

| Date published | Number of proposals | Number of (net) closures proposed |
|---|---|---|
| Pre January 1 1985 | 10 | 21 |
| January – March | 3 | 4 |
| April – June | 21 | 10 |
| July – September | 10 | 12 |
| October – January 1986 | 14 | 20 |
| TOTAL | 58* | 67 |

* from 27 different authorities

Source: Audit Commission analysis of information supplied by DES, March 1986.

Exhibit 6

## PLANNED ADJUSTMENTS TO SECONDARY SCHOOL CAPACITY

### LEA plans as at mid-1985

*SAMPLE OF 46 LEAs*

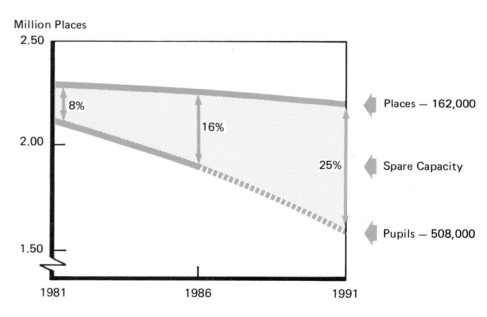

Source: Audit Commission analysis of Auditors' reports, 1986

24. In short, all the evidence suggests that an opportunity potentially critical to the future quality of secondary education is going begging. Yet the experience of many authorities indicates that given the local will, progress is possible. The Commission's auditors have drawn the attention of authorities to the scale of the local opportunities. For a typical authority the cost implications in 1991 of failing to take action to reorganise its secondary schools could well be in the order of £6 million per annum (at 1985 prices). And its earlier report suggested how these might be progressed. A robust method of accurate population forecasting is required; the LEA must check its existing building stock, and ensure that its method of measuring capacity is appropriate. There should be a clear definition of who is responsible for the reviews, and the role (if any) of departments other than education

should be specified. Full information on all the available options should be made available to the decision-makers. Clear decision criteria should be established by LEAs when undertaking reviews, taking in both educational and financial factors. The financial appraisals should be "broad brush"; it is more useful to be roughly right than precisely wrong. But all the key variables should be included with an assessment of their sensitivity. A timetable and frequency of review should be established, with a timescale which is appropriate to the problem being tackled – taking into account the length of the consultation procedures.

25. The first step is to establish a project team to conduct the reviews. Obvious as this may seem, around one LEA in four has yet to take this essential first step. The Commission considers that the staff work is most appropriately assigned to an inter-departmental working party led by a senior officer from the education department. Of course, this team will not undertake the work in isolation from members, since they will have regular contact with them – and in any case regular progress reviews should be arranged. The review team will need to include senior officers from the authority's property and finance functions. Reviews of school accommodation cannot be undertaken in isolation from a wider evaluation of the authority's total future needs for buildings. Geographical, demographic and sometimes social constraints in addition to the basic educational considerations may limit the range of options for detailed consideration. Nevertheless, all procedures should ensure that a wide view is taken, when any action is under consideration, of the authority's needs and of the alternative future uses of surplus buildings. And it will be essential for the financial implications of the various options to be examined thoroughly.

26. The following steps are essential to any review of local options for secondary school organisations:

(i)   Determine the nature and extent of the potential problem for the authority as a whole, making a range of assumptions about key demand variables such as new local housing development, staying-on rates and so forth. These will need to be shown on a division by division or town by town basis.

(ii)  Determine the cost of doing nothing in financial and educational terms, before any options are considered.

(iii) Agree in advance the main decision criteria. These will almost certainly need to be a mixture of educational and logistics, e.g. maximum and minimum sizes for particular classes, acceptable maximum travelling distances and times.

(iv)  Identify and cost the main options. In addition to all the normal teaching and non-teaching costs, the evaluation should take account of the opportunity cost of continuing to occupy the building and grounds (i.e. what the property might be worth to another user), and the value of any out of school uses to which the buildings are put.

(v)   Evaluate the options both in educational and financial terms, taking into account the possible risks (e.g. that demand may not be as projected, for given reasons) and the timing of changes, calculating the net present value or revenue profiles of the various choices.

27. Neither DES nor the Chartered Institute of Public Finance and Accountancy (CIPFA) has developed a standard framework for costing the range of options available to LEAs facing falling school rolls. Exhibit 7, drawn from the Commission's earlier report, shows some of the non-teaching costs to be taken into account. All the potential costs, with the exception of home-to-school transport are "one off"; all the savings are recurring with the sole exception of capital receipts. The figures included in

Exhibit 7

## FINANCIAL IMPLICATIONS OF METHODS OF REMOVING SURPLUS PLACES

| METHOD OF REMOVING SURPLUS PLACES | POTENTIAL SAVINGS | POTENTIAL COSTS |
|---|---|---|
| Premises closure/disposals through school closures or amalgamations | All premises costs eliminated<br><br>Some savings in teaching and support staff costs — by avoiding the dis-economies of small schools<br><br>Capital receipts generated if schools can be sold | Administrative burden eg. publications of notices, public meetings etc<br><br>Home-to-school transport costs will increase to some extent<br><br>Possible redundancy costs |
| Alternative use of schools | All premises costs are transferred to new user — provided that full costs are identified and an economic charge is levied | |
| Mothballing whole schools | All premises costs — except for basic maintenance and rates | Mothballing costs |
| Piecemeal mothballing of schools | Savings mostly from:—<br>(i) Fuel and light — if heating systems are zoned so as not to heat certain areas (£175 per room per annum)<br>(ii) Cleaning assistance (£250 per room per annum)<br><br>Small savings from decorating and maintenance costs (£75 per room per annum) | |
| Removal of temporary accommodation | Fuel and light — temporary units usually have high energy consumption costs, typically five times that of permanent accommodation<br><br>Repairs and maintenance<br><br>Cleaning assistance<br><br>Income (if the temporary units can be sold) | Removal costs |

Source: Audit Commission, 1984

financial appraisals do not necessarily need to be very detailed or precise. In some examples, the figures seen have perhaps been too precise; the requirement is for an approach which quantifies the key variables and assesses their sensitivity. LEAs should, therefore, be able to improve practice in this area from within their existing staffing resources. With the options clearly spelled out and evaluated in educational and financial terms, members will be able to reach informed judgements as to the course to be followed taking all relevant local factors into account. The Commission recognises that there are those who would rather not be "confused by the facts". But the scale of the problem and the unacceptable consequences of failure to act make this approach no longer tenable – if indeed it ever was.

28. The *Education Act* of 1980 sets out the statutory steps necessary to effect reorganisation of the schools and reduction of intakes in respect of the closure or amalgamation of schools. Public notice needs to be given where it is intended to reduce admissions to a school by one fifth or more. Very thorough and time-consuming local consultation regarding any proposed school closures is required with governors, parents, church authorities (in the case of voluntary schools), teachers and local community. Nearly all LEA proposals for closure meet with substantial local opposition. Nobody likes change; protest costs the protester little and losses affect a few profoundly whereas the benefits are spread over all local ratepayers. The experience of auditors over the past 12 months is that success in "carrying" unpopular reorganisation proposals requires the following:

(a) Sound staff work on likely capacity/demand imbalances. It is the general experience that protesters almost invariably begin by denying that the problem exists. All the numbers and critical assumptions will be challenged. Mistakes are expensive; and it pays to err on the side of optimism (i.e. giving potential opponents of change the benefit of any legitimate doubt that may exist). It also pays to be very explicit about the critical assumptions made, so that these can be discussed openly and rationally.

(b) A comprehensive rather than piecemeal approach, so that the support of potential beneficiaries of changes can be enlisted to counterbalance the inevitable protests and to provide those concerned with a broad perspective.

(c) "Open government". Rumours are almost invariably more damaging than reality. While some CEOs and LEAs consider that providing the general public with information prior to decisions may lead to misuse of the data as well as possible "planning blight" on those schools perceived to be threatened, the Commission believes that there are considerable advantages to an open, staged approach. For example:
 – releasing a discussion paper outlining the problem and the costs of doing nothing;
 – holding a series of local meetings at which those involved are invited to put forward options for dealing with the situation;
 – publishing the decision criteria before any detailed options are developed;
 – publishing the full range of options with the cost and educational implications spelled out for discussion at local meetings before the LEA has decided what course to adopt.

(d) Incentives to encourage the acceptance of the changes. In some, at least a share (e.g. 30 per cent) of the capital receipts from the disposal of surplus buildings is given back to the education committee, whereas in others, capital receipts go into a central "pool" and are lost to the education committee.

(e) Diversion to alternative uses of the whole or large parts of schools is fairly common, e.g. use by further education, day centres for the elderly, magistrates court accommodation. But the associated costs which are incurred as a result need to be quantified (including the opportunity cost) so that members are aware of the costs of their decisions. The DES Architects and Buildings Group has published a number of useful broadsheets on the alternative use of school buildings.

\* \* \*

The primary purpose of closing schools is not financial – although the savings on maintaining, cleaning and heating buildings could eventually be of the order of £150 – 200 million a year. Rather, local reorganisation is usually necessary to enhance the quality of education, by making the best possible use of teachers' skills. Another prerequisite for making the best possible use of teachers' skills is that each school should be appropriately staffed. The next section therefore discusses an approach to allocating teacher complements (i.e. numbers) to schools that goes beyond the application of crude pupil : teacher ratios (PTRs).

**ALLOCATING TEACHING RESOURCES TO SCHOOLS**

29. The sizes of classes vary widely for pupils in the same age range, as Exhibit 8 indicates. When a staff complement, or indeed any kind of budget, is to be set, the process starts with two elements: a statement of resource needs, often based on an assembly of bids from the departments or groups who are to apply the resource and a statement of the resources which are available. If there is a discrepancy between these two, the process of setting the complement involves striking a balance between them.

Exhibit 8

**ENGLISH SECONDARY SCHOOL CLASS SIZES IN JANUARY 1984**

**% classes taught by one teacher**

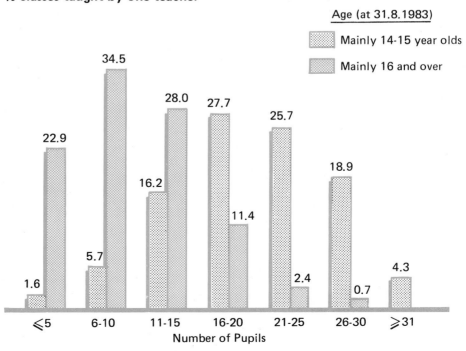

Source: Department of Education and Science, 1985

The choice to be made is between providing fewer resources than are perceived to be needed in order to stay within the level of resources available, or making available more resources in order to meet the full perceived need or reaching some compromise between the two. The process by which LEAs set staff complements for secondary schools generally follows this pattern although the levels of provision proposed and ultimately decided on differ significantly between LEAs as Table 5 based on CIPFA estimates demonstrates.

Table 5: PUPIL: TEACHER RATIOS IN SECONDARY SCHOOLS
January 1985

|  | Lowest | Highest | Average |
|---|---|---|---|
| Shire counties | 15.0:1 | 18.1 | 16.4 |
| Metropolitan districts | 13.8 | 16.8 | 15.5 |
| Outer London boroughs | 11.3 | 16.9 | 13.9 |

30. The Commission is concerned to observe that the assignment of teachers (and thus presumably educational quality) varies so widely. To correct the present apparently haphazard basis for assigning teachers to schools:

(i) PTRs should be abandoned as the basis for allocating teacher numbers to schools, since these ignore the nature of the curriculum to be delivered and mask over- and under-staffing; At present it is as though general hospitals were staffed solely according to the number of beds rather than, as is the case, taking account of the medical and surgical specialities available. However, LEAs will need to retain some form of overall control over the number of teachers employed, and PTRs are useful in this context.

(ii) Activity-led staffing should form the basis for setting teaching staff complements for schools and should thereby ensure that staffing levels are compatible with the agreed curriculum.

The rationale for each of these steps is discussed further below.

**Abandon pupil : teacher ratios as a basis for staffing**

31. A widespread weakness of the process for setting teacher complements is the form in which LEAs' staffing requirements are stated. The statement of staffing requirements normally centres on a PTR. This number, which is determined by a mixture of professional judgement, financial expediency and historical inertia is simply divided into the number of pupils to give the level of staffing for each school. The origins of the PTR are normally lost in the mists of time, and it is rarely adjusted. Some authorities make use of different PTRs for different age groups of pupils; the ranges of PTRs used for the initial allocation of staff to schools for different age groups found in an earlier study by Walsh* et al were:

| Age group | PTR ranges |
|---|---|
| Years 1 – 3 | 1:19 – 1:23 |
| Years 4 – 5 | 1:15 – 1:18 |
| Sixth form | 1:10 – 1:14 |

The range implies differences of 20 per cent (or more in the case of sixth forms) in school staffing for a similar number of pupils. But many authorities do not even differentiate the PTR by year group, still less by type of school; they use a single PTR for all pupils aged between 11 and 16.

---

* *Falling School Rolls and the Management of the Teaching Profession*, Walsh, Dunne, Stoten and Stewart. NFER–Nelson 1984. ISBN 0 7005 0663 2

32. Since the needs of pupils and schools are not solely the result of the number of pupils, the application of PTRs leads to anomalies. Where the anomalies cause a failure to meet an identifiable need, an extra staffing allocation is sought and commonly met. For instance, additional allocations are made in order to meet individual needs and circumstances, such as the integration of handicapped pupils into ordinary schools or the problems of split sites. In one of the authorities visited by the Commission's study team, the following additions to the basic allowance were applied:

- Split site: two to five teachers depending on the needs of individual schools;
- Disruptive pupils: two or three teachers to be used at the discretion of the head teacher;
- Social priority: addition based upon an index of social deprivation;
- TVEI: there are five schools involved in the Technical and Vocational Education Initiative sharing a total of 8.2 teachers;
- Teacher-counsellors: five schools each having one post – the remnant of an experiment which was not extended;
- Immigrants/ethnic minorities: allocation based upon numbers of such children.

In some authorities, additional allocations are also made as a result of special pleading by individual heads and advisers. But the PTR is the major basis of staffing for schools, and as financial cuts have affected LEAs, fewer of the ad hoc additions mentioned above have been included in staff complements.

33. If an anomaly of the PTR allocation leads to an unintended improvement of provision, the anomaly is seldom identified. As an example, consider a school with a growing roll in an LEA which staffs secondary school first years according to a PTR of 1 : 19. If the school has an extra 19 pupils in the first year, then it will get an extra teacher. But the extra pupils may not have required the formation of an extra class, being absorbed in existing class groups, and therefore may not fully take up the time of the extra teacher. The school has an increase in staff resources per class of pupils which can then be used, for example, to increase provision for the school's management or for pupil counselling.

34. There is also a difficulty in using the same PTR for all sizes of school. Smaller schools, if they are to be able to deliver the same curriculum, need proportionally more staff because:

(a) There are certain fixed staffing costs, such as the need for a head teacher and a basic spread of teacher skills.
(b) Schools need to be of a certain basic size if their subject departments are to warrant the appointment of some teachers on higher as well as some on lower salary scales.
(c) Groups cannot be formed as efficiently, particularly for remedial pupils, in smaller schools.

In the early 1970s, the Scottish Education Department found the relationship between staffing and the size of school, shown in Exhibit 9 (overleaf). It is based upon a secondary school staffing model and evidence from a staffing survey. More recently HMI have evaluated the PTR required to deliver a curriculum consistent with the recommendations contained in the White Paper *Better Schools*. Both analyses indicate that the unit staffing requirements begin to rise very rapidly as pupil numbers fall below about 800.

Exhibit 9

**RELATIONSHIP BETWEEN ROLL OF SCHOOL AND
PUPIL : TEACHER RATIO — COMPREHENSIVE SCHOOLS**

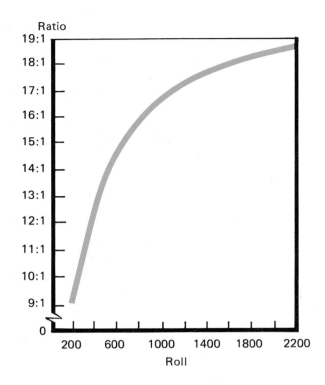

Source: Scottish Education Department
Audit Commission analysis of DES data

35. Thus, using PTRs as a basis for apportioning teacher complements to schools weakens authorities' scope to manage effectively. In particular, the use of a PTR fails to show the increase in staffing needs as schools become smaller and thereby deprives authorities of a signal of the need to close schools as pupil numbers fall. And the ratio gives no idea of the level of educational provision in schools: only the teaching input is described. Worst of all, perhaps, the PTR is regarded as evidence that the quality of education is improving; an "improvement" (i.e. reduction) in the PTR is regarded as evidence that the quality of education is improving; a "worsening" (i.e. increase) indicates the reverse. In fact, over England and Wales overall, the pupil teacher ratio has been steadily "improving" over the past five years. Some LEAs have grasped this as a ready pretext for failing to examine the underlying realities of staffing in individual schools and have been content to argue that the quality of education must be improving because the PTR is becoming progressively "better". There is, though, no evidence of which the Commission is aware that, within very broad limits (i.e. + or − 20 per cent) the PTR affects the quality of education or the results achieved, taking account of appropriate adjustments for demographic and social conditions. And, within the EEC, France and West Germany have a "worse" PTR than that in England and Wales. One consequence of LEAs' preoccupation with PTRs is that target PTRs are very seldom altered; the full effects of fluctuations in the education budget are therefore imposed on expenditure heads other than teacher salaries, such as in-service training, building maintenance or books and equipment.

36. Quite apart from the near term problems involved in using PTRs as a basis for school staffing, the ratio-based approach will result in very serious difficulties in the future. If teachers' numbers are linked to the number of pupils only, manpower planning will become much more difficult:

— Every year, some 12–13,000 teachers leave the profession through retirement or resignation; and 8,000 new graduates enter post graduate teacher training, although some of these would decide not to take up teaching appointments once they are qualified. (Surprisingly, no figures are readily available on the "drop out" rate following post graduate teaching courses).

— Over the next five years, the number of teachers required under the assumptions shown earlier will entail an annual net reduction of the order of 8–9,000. This is not far short of double the level over the last three years, when there has been an average annual net reduction in full-time equivalent teachers in post of some 3,900.

— In the next five years, there will need to be a net reduction of some 3–5,000 teachers a year over and above the historical levels of "natural" wastage, if PTRs are to be maintained. This will inevitably cause considerable disruption to teacher training establishments which have a current capacity to "produce" around 8,000 new teachers every year.

— But when rolls begin to increase in the early 1990s, there will need to be a continuing increase in recruitment as Exhibit 10 indicates. DES on the supply and education of teachers has estimated that no less than 14 per cent of all qualified graduates will be needed for teaching, more than double the current level.

Exhibit 10

**REQUIREMENT FOR NEW TEACHERS IN SECONDARY SCHOOLS, 1985-1999**
**England and Wales, '000**

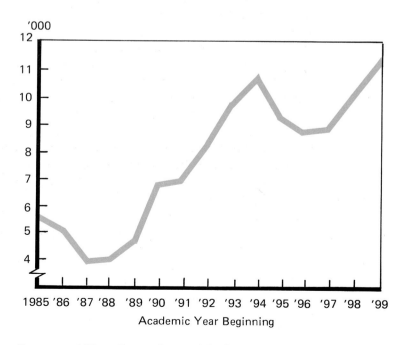

Source: ACSET: *Future Demand for Primary and Secondary School Teachers*, Table 10

In such circumstances, there is an obvious risk that quality standards will slip.

- There are obvious advantages in planning ahead using a curriculum-led staffing (see below) approach, so that competent teachers are not forced against their will to leave the profession in the next three to five years only for the LEA to be faced with the need for greatly increased recruitment in the early 1990s, which the teacher training system may not be able to meet.

\* \* \*

Thus, there are serious risks inherent in using PTRs as a basis for allocating teaching complements to individual schools. But it must be recognised that these weaknesses do not apply at the LEA level. If members are to retain control over teaching costs and avoid being "snowed" by educationalists, they will need to establish explicit planning guidelines for the authority as a whole, incorporating a target PTR and total revenue and capital expenditure. A cost-plus mentality is no more desirable in education than it is elsewhere.

**Substitute activity-led staffing (ALS)**

37. The response of some LEAs to the inadequacy of the PTR as a staffing method has been to adopt curriculum-led staffing (CLS). A curriculum-based approach to the setting of staff complements in the schools of an LEA does not imply the implementation of a model curriculum in individual schools. Head teachers' freedom to manage the curriculum need not be (and in practice has not been) reduced when staff complements are set by reference to a curriculum instead of by more traditional methods.

38. Curriculum-based staffing begins with a discussion of the shape and balance of the curriculum which leads on to a series of statements such as:

"History in the fourth year is to be taught for three periods a week in groups of no more than 25 pupils".

A full set of such curricular statements is considered and decided on by the authority following consultation between LEA officers, advisers and teachers; and this constitutes the curriculum model. The curriculum model is combined with the projected numbers of pupils in each year group in order to derive a projected number of taught periods required in each school. Once an allowance is made for teachers' duties other than classroom teaching, an estimate can be constructed of the staffing requirement of each school and, consequently of the LEA as a whole. The Appendix includes a fuller description of the build-up of a CLS model.

39. It has been LEAs' almost universal experience that the indicated need for teachers exceeds what the current allocation of money or total manpower complement will allow. Many LEAs have, as a result, abandoned the pursuit of CLS and continued to use PTR-based methods. This reaction stems from a limited understanding of the scope of CLS. As with any budget-setting process, the opening statements are just the beginning. If the judgement is that provision is to be less than the initial model calls for, the reduction should be achieved by adjusting the curricular provision from that indicated in the model. In the history example cited above, it might be that the maximum group size has to increase to 28. On the other hand, the decision might be that all teachers will have to have less time available for vocational guidance to pupils in years four and five. *The use of CLS thus entails no assumption that the authority should set staff complements more or less generously, nor does it require that complements should match educationalists' assessment of staffing needs.* It is a tool to inform the process, by referring staffing to an intermediate output of

education (the curriculum) instead of to an input (the PTR).

Exhibit 11 shows that the use of CLS need not imply a need for resources over those indicated by the PTR (which is currently 15.8 : 1 for comprehensive schools). The indicated staffing complement can be brought into line with the available resources by adjusting the curriculum choice, changing the constraints on group size or increasing the contact ratio as discussed below.

Exhibit 11

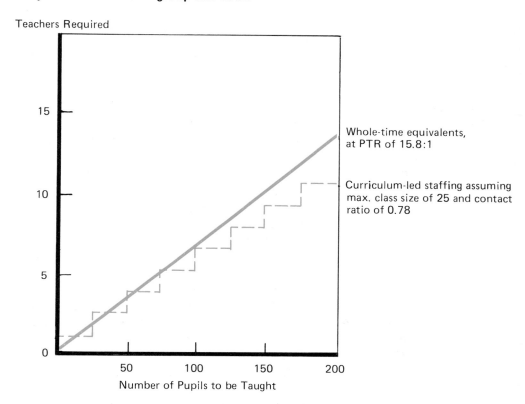

**EFFECTS OF PUPIL : TEACHER RATIO AND CURRICULUM-LED STAFFING APPROACHES**
**Subject with maximum group size of 25**

*ILLUSTRATIVE*

Teachers Required

Whole-time equivalents, at PTR of 15.8:1

Curriculum-led staffing assuming max. class size of 25 and contact ratio of 0.78

Number of Pupils to be Taught

40. CLS thus has clear advantages over the PTR as a basis for setting teaching complements for schools. It provides the basis for a clearer understanding between parents on the one hand and the LEA on the other as to what will be taught in local schools; some authorities (e.g. Croydon) have developed an explicit contract setting out what will be taught to different age groups and what attainments parents are entitled to expect. Secondly, the CLS process illustrates clearly the options about what is to be foregone as a result of a shortfall of financial resources; and it allows for a rational allocation of teaching staff to schools which takes account of the differing needs of schools of different size and type.

41. There is no doubt that CLS represents a considerable improvement over current PTR-based methods, although relatively few LEAs have adopted the approach: according to the latest expenditure policy survey of HMI, 18 authorities out of 104 say that they have an agreed curriculum that can be used for staffing purposes and 10 say that they have actually implemented a CLS policy. However, it involves making an allowance for teachers' duties other than classroom teaching. That allowance is normally expressed in terms of a contact ratio (the proportion of timetabled hours

that a teacher spends in front of a class). Table 6 shows average teacher contact ratio for each of the categories of education authority, shire counties, metropolitan districts and London authorities. In each case the authorities with the lowest and highest contact ratios are listed and the average is shown. For example, an average teacher in Avon in 1985 would spend 76.5 per cent of timetabled hours in class.

*Table 6:* AVERAGE CONTACT RATIOS IN 1985.
% timetabled hours in class – all teachers including heads and deputy heads

|  | Lowest | Highest | Average |
|---|---|---|---|
| Shire counties | 76.5% (Avon) | 81.8 (Isle of Wight) | 78.3 |
| Met. districts | 73.0 (Manchester) | 80.4 (Kirklees) | 77.2 |
| London | 69.3 (ILEA) | 79.2 (Bexley) | 73.2 |

Source: Data supplied by DES

Thus, a teacher in ILEA teaches on average 5.2 fewer lessons per week than a teacher in the Isle of Wight (assuming a 40-period week). In national terms a change in the contact ratio from 78 to 80 per cent would lead to a reduction of some 5,900 in the number of teachers required; these would represent annual costs of some £72 million.

42. The Commission does not take a view on what would be an appropriate contact ratio for secondary school teachers. Its concern, arising from observation of practice in the participating authorities, is that in too many LEAs the contact ratio is a residual outcome of other decisions rather than the result of explicit choice. At the time when curriculum models are being drawn up prior to the setting of staff complements, authorities should consider explicitly the activities other than classroom teaching which teachers need to discharge during the school day. Four main classes of activity are immediately identifiable:

(a) School based activities: those relating to each school and which will not vary greatly with the size of school, for example: policy decision making, external relations, LEA and government returns.

(b) Teacher-based activities: those relating to individual teachers, for example:
  – substitution for absent staff;
  – appointment of staff;
  – timetable creation and maintenance;
  – lesson preparation;
  – in-service training and induction of new teachers.

(c) Pupil-related activities, for example:
  – record keeping;
  – reports and references;
  – pastoral and disciplinary work;
  – marking and individual follow-up work.

(d) Other classes of activity may be identified, e.g. site related activities: those necessarily resulting from a split school site, community or area related activities, where there is a separate community role for a school or where social deprivation locally is considered to warrant extended pastoral work by teachers.

The incorporation of an explicit estimate of teacher effort outside the classroom into the CLS process extends that process into *activity-led staffing* (ALS). An illustration of ALS is shown in the Appendix.

43. The introduction of full ALS would remove much of the current need for additions to the staffing above what LEAs' stated policies provide for.

But no formula can cover all eventualities; so some staff are always likely to be allocated above the numbers which the policy prescribes. Where this happens, an LEA should be clear that the need being catered for is one which will actually be helped by the allocation of extra teaching staff. For example, in some cases it may be that extra support staff may be more relevant. Any allocation of teaching staff to schools above the number determined by an LEA's staffing policy should be made on a basis clearly stated before the staffing process begins. Where possible, need should be measured.

44. ALS can also be helpful in determining, systematically, the need for non-teaching staff who provide direct support to teachers as well as help in running the school as a whole. An inappropriate level of support can have a marked effect on the productivity of teachers as reflected in their contact ratios. The Audit Commission report on non-teaching costs in secondary schools mentioned points schemes as a possible starting point for the allocation of support staff. Visits to LEAs and schools during the course of that study showed a wide variety of approach to the allocation of support staff – as well as wide variation in the levels of staff. Some kind of points system was common; but there were LEAs which did not use them. Formulae for the calculation of points also varied widely: examples included derivations based on the number of pupils on roll, on age weighting unrelated to that used for Burnham unit totals, on Burnham unit totals themselves, on unit totals in use before the Houghton report, and on the Burnham group of the school.

45. This variety of approach indicates that there is no common understanding of what actually leads to the need for technicians or administrative support. The proper process for allocating support staff to schools should parallel that of ALS proposed for teacher staffing. The need for laboratory technicians, CDT technicians, and library assistants should be based on the needs as described by a curriculum model. An assessment should be made of the technician effort required to deliver that curriculum, and it may be that assessment is based on professional judgement alone. Even so, a professional judgement of what needs to be done on the ground is far superior to an arbitrary formula.

46. Finally, the ALS approach can be used to assess the effects on staffing requirements of various ways of organising the schools within an LEA. The principles of the assessment are simple: any proposed organisation of schools implies the pupil numbers in each school in each year. Application of ALS to these numbers yields staffing requirements under the proposed organisation. ALS could also illustrate the global relationships between school capacity and staffing levels. At present, there is no implementation of ALS which will yield actual figures and the next best evidence is that provided by CLS which assumes a uniform contact ratio in all schools, whatever their size. Exhibit 12 (overleaf) illustrates the relationship between school capacity and teacher staffing by reference to curriculum models compatible with the recommendations of the White Paper, *Better Schools*. The staffing requirement is expressed in terms of the ratio of pupils to teachers which results from the provision of the stated curriculum in the schools of the stated sizes.

47. The sizes of schools are described in forms-of-entry, which is a unit of 30 pupils. Clearly, with different curricular assumptions, the economies of scale will be different. The view of the Government, expressed in *Better Schools,* and that of HMI is that it is educationally disadvantageous for comprehensive secondary schools to have fewer than six forms-of-entry which is equivalent to 90 pupils for a school serving pupils aged 11 – 16 and appreciably more than that for schools for 11 – 18 year olds.

Exhibit 12

## PUPIL : TEACHER RATIO TO DELIVER A 'BETTER SCHOOLS' CURRICULUM

**Analysis by number of forms of entry (30 pupils)**

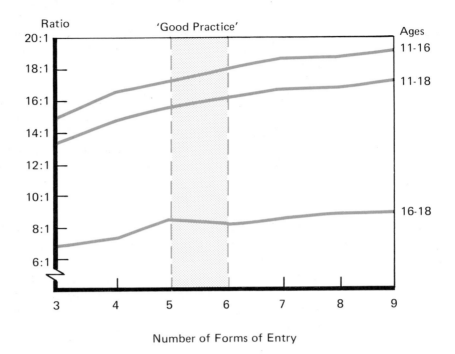

Number of Forms of Entry

Source: HMI

Exhibit 13

## SURPLUS CAPACITY IN SECONDARY SCHOOLS
**Number of Schools in Different Ranges**

*NORTHERN CITY EXAMPLE*

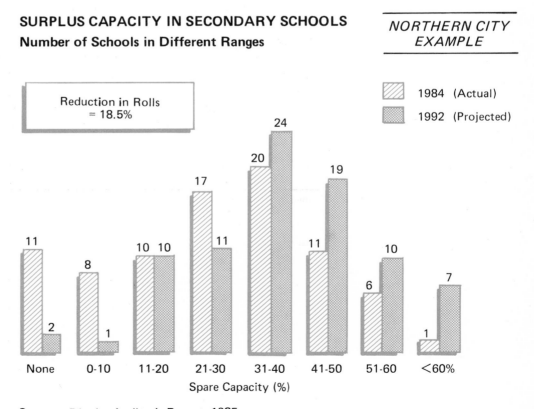

Spare Capacity (%)

Source: District Auditor's Report, 1985

48. Thus, economic considerations and professional educational judgements alike point to a need for school systems to be reorganised to avoid schools below the six forms-of-entry threshold. In January 1985, DES statistics show that about 1,790 comprehensive schools out of a total of 4,382 had fewer than 800 pupils. Although some of these will not be catering for the full 11 – 16 age range, it seems certain that a very large number of schools will be too small to be viable educationally. The situation is certain to worsen since, as Exhibit 13 (based on the situation in a northern metropolitan district) illustrates, school overcapacity is going to increase. An alternative approach open to an authority is to go against the professional views of the Inspectorate and others and respond to demands that schools should be deliberately made small with the aim of maintaining communities on a more human scale. The extent of the required narrowing of the curriculum could be illustrated by curriculum models. Such models would not however show the disadvantages of the wide variations in ability within classes which are an inevitable feature of small schools.

**IMPLEMENTING STAFF COMPLEMENTS IN INDIVIDUAL SCHOOLS**

49. Once an authority has determined the teacher staffing required in each school, it needs to take steps to ensure that each school actually has the staffing which has been determined. As school rolls fall, the changes in staff complements may be too substantial to be achieved solely by natural wastage. If one teacher is left in a school surplus to the complement determined for that school, the cost of employing that teacher [perhaps £12,000 – 15,000 a year including pension contributions] is so much money misdirected at the school where he or she is employed. If this holding of the teacher surplus to requirements results in another school being short of staff, there is a concomitant educational loss to that other school.

50. The Commission's fieldwork in 12 authorities revealed considerable variations in approach. Two were unable to provide any information on over- and under-staffing in the schools – a problem that is discussed later. A further four negotiated staffing with schools in such a way that the target establishment could always be reached either by providing justification for the extra staffing within the staffing policy, or in one case, redeploying designated teachers to a central supply pool for one year, so that no over- or under-staffing occurred. In the remaining six authorities, in 1984–85, 22 per cent of the schools were overstaffed and 10 per cent were understaffed according to local policy. Only four LEAs visited were able to provide detailed information on how many teachers were provided in excess:

*Table 7:* OVER- AND UNDER-STAFFING IN SECONDARY SCHOOLS, 1984–5.
         Four fieldwork LEAs

| | |
|---|---|
| Number of teacher posts | |
| – Above agreed establishments | 79 |
| – Vacant | 27.3 |
| Cost implications | |
| – Overstaffing | £970,000/year |
| – Unfilled vacancies | £336,000 |

51. It is therefore important that authorities should make full use of all the means at their disposal for implementing staff complements and should monitor closely the extent of variation in staffing levels from those indicated by authority policies. The range of measures which authorities should use in addition to natural wastage (i.e. normal retirements and resignations) to adjust teacher numbers comprises:

(i)   Redeployment of teachers from one school to another.
(ii)  More use of part-time teachers.
(iii) Recruitment from as broad a field as possible.
(iv)  Early retirement.
(v)   Voluntary severance.

LEAs need to choose which combination of measures to use in particular cases. They are listed above in descending order of their desirability: the granting of early retirement or voluntary severance has the effect of wasting investment in the development of a teacher's skills.

**Redeployment**

52. The White Paper *Teaching Quality* (Cmnd 8836) states in commenting on the decline in pupil and teacher numbers, that "The most powerful single instrument available to authorities may be the redeployment of teachers from one school to another" and that "redeployment should be part of a planned approach to school staffing, and not an option of last resort. . .". It presses the argument that redeployment should be more widely used to ensure that the teaching force was appropriately deployed. The White Paper understates the importance of careful manpower planning and the opportunities available from careful use of natural wastage (i.e. normal resignations and retirements) of around 12,000 teachers a year, to adjust school staffing levels.

53. Redeployment clearly has an important role to play in helping LEAs to adjust to falling rolls and to manage the problem of "mismatch" of teaching qualifications and experience referred to earlier. Where necessary, teachers can be moved from schools where there is no surplus of staff in order to improve the match between subjects taught and teachers' qualifications. For instance, suppose that the position at three schools is as follows:

School A:   One vacancy, for a modern languages teacher
School B:   One teacher above complement, with the geography department identified as able to shed a member of staff
School C:   Modern languages department overstaffed and geography department short of one member of staff.

In this case, two teachers should be redeployed – a geographer from B to C and a modern linguist from C to A. Such redeployment has been termed "knock-on" redeployment.

54. All LEAs have agreements for the redeployment of teachers. These agreements usually contain protection for individual teachers against further redeployment for a period of time, usually two to four years, a right of return to the original school if a suitable vacancy occurs, the payment of excess travelling expenses and protection of salary level. The operation of redeployment varies from one LEA to another. But the process generally begins after May 31, the last resignation date for teachers before the end of the school year. By this date the number of vacancies and surpluses in schools is known with a high degree of accuracy. The problem is that the time available for redeployment is then very short. Officers and head teachers must do a great deal of work very quickly since, in most cases, the process must be completed before the summer holidays which normally start at the end of July.

55. The result of timing problems, and others, is that few teachers are redeployed. For example, in 1984–85, one authority taking part in the study redeployed 21 secondary teachers voluntarily and none compulsorily, even though this resulted in 33 secondary schools remaining above their official staffing establishment. Another authority redeployed five secondary teachers voluntarily and one compulsorily in the same year whilst 13 schools were overstaffed. Table 8 (opposite) shows the minimal extent of redeployment of teachers in the study authorities as a whole.

*Table 8:* TEACHERS REDEPLOYED
% Teachers in post at January – 9 sample authorities

|  | 1982–83 | 1983–84 | 1984–85 |
|---|---|---|---|
| Voluntary | 0.24% | 0.35 | 0.27 |
| Compulsory | 0.43 | 0.52 | 0.66 |

If it proves impossible to redeploy a teacher, he or she remains surplus to agreed staffing levels. In some cases no redeployment takes place during the school year, so that the teacher will stay as surplus throughout the academic year.

56. In addition, the study team found examples of posts not being filled as a result of failure to redeploy teachers. These included important posts. A number of obstacles to redeployment were identified:
- Redeployment is a difficult process. It takes up a great deal of time both for head teachers and LEA officers.
- Potential recipients of redeployees often suspect that head teachers of schools with teachers above complement put forward only less able teachers for nomination.
- The status of voluntary schools causes particular problems: governors of the school have the power to block redeployment into the school.
- Redeployment is unpopular with teachers and is considered by some to damage morale.

57. The problem in teacher redeployment in secondary schools must be solved if teacher numbers are to be kept at the complements set by LEAs' staffing policies. The following steps help:
(i) Begin the redeployment process earlier. This may on occasion require provisional nominations to be made for compulsory redeployment, some of which may eventually be cancelled if resignations obviate the need for the redeployment.
(ii) Base the choice of nominee primarily on curriculum and school need after taking cognizance of personal circumstances. In no case should the final choice of redeployee rest entirely with the school which has to lose a teacher.
(iii) Make new appointments to the service of the authority and include an explicit statement that a teacher may be required to move where necessary. Teachers (other than those in voluntary schools) are employed by their LEA and not by individual schools, even where the appointment of the teacher is to an individual school. This position would be emphasised by a provision in the 1986 Education Bill that appointment and dismissal of staff at schools other than voluntary aided schools should be under the control of the LEA.
(iv) Ensure that redeployment is used for all grades of teacher. At present most authorities restrict the use of redeployment to teachers on the lowest grade.
(v) Assist teachers to travel longer distances, or possibly move house, e.g. with more generous travel allowances and removal expenses provision.

58. When redeployment becomes a standard practice, much of its present unpopularity can be removed, as a direct result of dispelling the mistaken impression amongst some heads and teachers that it is a special measure restricted to less competent teachers. Some of the measures proposed here may appear harsh in terms of choice given to teachers. That is to some extent counter-balanced by improvements in morale, particularly in schools which would otherwise be understaffed or where some individual teachers would obviously be under-employed.

**More use of part-time teachers**

59. The use of part-time teachers can add greatly to flexibility in the face of uncertainties over the curriculum and local school rolls, as the experience of many further education colleges (where part-time lecturers often account for 20 – 25 per cent of full-time equivalent academic staff) demonstrates. However, the proportion of teaching carried out by part-time teachers has diminished since the mid–1970s and currently stands at about 4 per cent. The size of part-timers' contribution is generally a matter for head teachers' decision since few LEAs restrict the extent which schools may employ teachers on part-time contracts. Some LEAs do however place restrictions on the contracts of employment which may be offered to part-time teachers such as requiring that the contracts be temporary.

Amongst the schools visited during the Special Study the proportion of teaching provided by part-time teachers varied from zero to 13 per cent. A major influence on the extent of use of part-time teachers was the local availability of candidates for this work. The availability of candidates also affected the degree to which the school could insist that a part-time teacher should work at times to suit the school.

60. Increased use of part-time teachers can bring considerable benefits. In particular, they can help to make good some of the shortage of teachers in scarcity subjects. Part-time teachers can also provide an easily tapped source of good quality cover for other teachers' absence. Head teachers pointed out to the Commission's team that unlike other casual supply teachers, a school's own part-timers are familiar with the school. This familiarity increases their effectiveness as supply teachers.

61. The principal obstacle to the use of part-time teachers which heads cited to the team is the difficulty of involving them in duties other than classroom teaching. A pastoral responsibility, for example, may require the teacher to be "on-call" throughout school hours. One advantage of ALS is that it makes explicit, quantified, provision for non-classroom duties. Once a judgement has been made of which duties part-time teachers could (and could not) appropriately discharge, time to discharge those duties can be allocated.

62. In order to help schools to make best use of part-timers, LEAs should consider the following steps:

   (i)   Offer permanent contracts of employment (except to part-time teachers whose posts are truly temporary) so as to provide continuity of teaching.
   (ii)  Include part-timers in redeployment agreements.
   (iii) Subject to appropriate minima, use variable hours contracts, thereby reducing the need for recruitment and redeployment as teacher complements change from year to year.
   (iv)  Wherever possible, require that the times at which the teacher is to teach are to be as directed by the school.

63. The supply of part-time teachers, particularly of those who are known to fit well in a particular school, can be enhanced by a greater incidence of stepping down from full to part-time. Current pension regulations do not in fact penalise teachers for stepping down: they lose the appropriate fraction of years of service but otherwise their pension calculation remains unchanged. However, the study team came upon a number of cases where teachers, their representatives or LEA officers did not realise that this was the case and assumed that a move to part-time work carried an unacceptable penalty in terms of pension. More positive publicity needs to be given, either by LEAs or by DES, to the possibilities of moving to part-time work.

Whilst the current regulations are in fact neutral in relation to stepping down to part-time, government could consider whether a positive incentive would be beneficial. It is already changing the regulations in relation to stepping down to a lower grade (as mentioned in the section on early retirement below), and might consider a parallel change in relation to part-time work.

**Broad field for recruitment**

64. Many LEAs operate some kind of "ring fence" as part of their recruitment procedures, to minimise the need for compulsory redundancies as school rolls fall. Typically the advertising of each vacancy is initially limited to teachers within the authority who have been nominated for redeployment and then to other teachers already within the employ of the authority. Only when the authority is satisfied that a suitable recruit cannot be found from either of these groups is a national advertisement permitted.

65. However, there is no doubt that a ring fence policy is educationally disadvantageous. It reduces the transfer of experience and innovation between authorities. And it restricts the choice of candidates and consequently reduces the quality of appointments. In one school visited by the study team, two vacancies had been filled by applicants who were the *only* applicants from within the LEA for the posts. Advertisement outside the LEA had not been permitted and the head teacher was dissatisfied with the resulting appointments.

66. It may not be realistic to expect authorities to abandon ring fences at a time when they have large numbers of teachers whom they need to redeploy away from their present schools; but the harmful effects of ring fences can be mitigated by the following steps:

(i) Carry out regular reviews of categories of post to be excluded from the ring fence. It is already common for headships to be excluded. By negotiation, other categories of post could be excluded where it is established that few suitable internal applicants are likely to be available.

(ii) Negotiate a procedure for exempting individual vacancies from the ring fence where those individual vacancies are not likely to be able to be filled internally, e.g. because there is a local shortage of teachers of the subject in question.

67. One school's recruit is often another's resignation. Recruitment would also be easier, therefore, if the present restrictions on resignation dates can be relaxed. At present there are three dates on which teachers in permanent service may leave their posts: December 31, April 30 and August 31. They correspond with the three major holidays of the school year. Notice of intention to resign at these dates has to be given two months before (or in the case of August, three months before) with head teachers being required to give one month notice longer than other teachers. This system ensures that new staff are in post for the start of a new term.

68. However, the system also tends to produce bunching of resignations with the consequence that the quality of recruitment is impaired by the haste of advertising and selection. At the same time, pupils may lose continuity in several subjects at once. These considerations argue for a removal of the present restrictions on resignation dates so that teachers' contracts of employment would require, say, three months' notice on either side. Such a change would have the additional advantage of facilitating a two-way flow of staff between teaching and other employment.

**Early retirement**

69. Increasing numbers of teachers have retired early since 1977 when it became possible to allow teachers with five or more years of reckonable service and who are aged 50 or more to retire and receive pension benefits immediately. In some authorities early retirement has become more common than retirement at the normal age. In one of the study authorities,

for example, this was the pattern of retirement during the past three years:

|  | 1982–83 | 1983–84 | 1984–85 |
|---|---|---|---|
| Normal retirements | 51 | 48 | 50 |
| Early retirements | 108 | 112 | 191 |

National figures for the corresponding period show a similar pattern: 1.6 per cent of teachers retired early in 1984–85 and a further 0.3 per cent retired at the normal retirement age. The comparable figures for 1982–83 were 1.2 per cent and 0.5 per cent respectively.

70. Early retirement serves to reduce teacher numbers, and to improve promotion prospects for younger teachers, while reducing the average age of the teaching force which some regard as desirable in itself. The drawback is that the substantial costs cancel out some of the salary savings, although present administrative arrangements obscure the extent of this. The costs incurred depend on whether the teacher retiring early is deemed to be retiring on the grounds of redundancy or in the interests of the efficiency of the education service. The effects on costs of granting early retirement to a teacher are shown in Exhibit 14, which also indicates where the gains and

Exhibit 14

**FINANCIAL IMPLICATIONS OF PREMATURE RETIREMENT**

| COST ELEMENT | WHERE THE GAIN/ LOSS FALLS |
|---|---|
| Basic pension paid early but at a lower level | Superannuation scheme |
| Basic retirement lump sum paid early but at a lower level | Superannuation scheme |
| Loss of LEA's contributions to superannuation scheme for years before normal retirement age | LEA's gain equal to Superannuation scheme's loss |
| Loss of teacher's contributions to superannuation scheme for years before normal retirement age | Superannuation scheme |
| Redundancy payment (retirement on grounds of redundancy only) | LEA and (until October 1986) Central Government |
| Enhancement of pension, if granted | LEA |
| Enhancement to retirement lump sum, if granted | LEA |
| Saving of teacher's salary | LEA |

losses fall. The superannuation scheme is a national superannuation scheme for teachers in all LEAs. Since decisions on early retirement are taken by LEAs, it is important to contrast the costs borne by them with the costs borne by the public sector as a whole. This distinction can be highlighted by reference to an illustrative example of a teacher aged 55, with 30 years' reckonable DES service, receiving a salary of £10,400. The LEA is assumed to be willing to grant the teacher five years' enhancement of pension. If the teacher lives to age 75, the present day equivalent value of all the savings and payments (net present value at 5 per cent) is shown in Table 9.

*Table 9:* NET PRESENT VALUE FROM EARLY RETIREMENT
£000, illustrative example

| | |
|---|---|
| Saving of salary and employer's share of employment charges | £98 |
| LEA's costs (before grant penalties) | (14) |
| LEA's net saving | 84 |
| Central contribution | (52) |
| Net public sector gain | 32 |

The value of the early retirement to the public sector as a whole is thus much less than the value of the salary and related savings because the costs of early retirement have cancelled out a large part of the savings.

71. Looked at strictly from the position of the LEA, the costs to the superannuation scheme and to the centre can be ignored. This makes early retirement look much more attractive because in effect the LEA is receiving a central subsidy. Even after the central subsidy, the financial value of the retirement is significantly less than the value of the saving of salary and employer's superannuation contribution. In some LEAs, the costs of enhancement are not charged to the education budget, although the education department and committee take decisions on early retirement. If this arrangement applied in the example here, the value of the premature retirement to the education budget is the full gross saving, £98,000.

72. This example shows the need for thorough costing of premature retirement cases before offers are made. In addition to the need for thorough consideration of costs, authorities should bear in mind a number of important points in the use of early retirement:

(i)  Decisions should be made as early as possible in the year so that adjustments to staffing can be made most advantageously. In one of the authorities visited during the course of the study, early retirement was used to adjust teacher numbers. When the authority faced financial difficulties, "special offers" were made at various times to reduce teacher numbers and costs further. In one case, a large number of early retirements were allowed at Christmas. This created considerable disruption of school timetables in the middle of the year.

(ii)  Schools and headteachers should be consulted before any individual is allowed to retire (although the Commission sees no need for a statutory duty to consult, such as the 1986 *Education Bill* would impose). In one authority visited in the study, there was no consultation at all: a head was told two weeks before the end of the autumn term that his head of chemistry was to retire from January 1st.

(iii)  Authorities should not use premature retirement to solve one problem [reducing teacher numbers] only to create a further difficulty, e.g. by exacerbating the situation in shortage subjects. In one LEA visited the number of premature retirements is determined annually. All teachers aged 50 and over are invited to apply if they wish to be considered. Successful applications are determined strictly by age – the oldest being allowed to retire early.

Government has already taken steps to encourage teachers who are approaching retirement to step down to a lower grade. This "premature retirement from grade" is the subject of regulations which the Secretary of State laid before Parliament in December 1985. At present, a teacher's pension is based on the best 365 consecutive days' salary in the last three years (1095 days) of service. The regulations allow for a similar rule to be applied to the last three years of service in the higher and lower grades separately.

**Voluntary severance**

73. LEAs might consider offering retainers to competent teachers who may wish to leave the profession temporarily, e.g. to raise a family, on condition that they return to teaching (perhaps on a part-time basis) in the early 1990s – thus obviating the need to recruit so many newly qualified teachers to meet the upturn in school rolls. In addition, there may be a case for offering voluntary severance to teachers below the minimum age for early retirement on terms which would be attractive and central government should give LEAs explicit powers to do so. Such a scheme would offer considerable cost advantages to the education service as well as mitigating the effect of early retirement on the age distribution of the teaching force. At present there is no such scheme for teachers, though individual authorities have investigated the possibility and there have been such schemes for other areas of the education service such as further education and the universities.

74. As with early retirement, the costs of voluntary severance would depend on the circumstances of the teacher to whom it was granted and the size of the redundancy payment which was given. As an illustration, if a teacher aged 40 with 15 years' reckonable service earning a salary of £10,400 lives to age 75 and is given a voluntary severance payment of £40,000, the financial value to the education service of the teacher's leaving is £102,000 – calculated on the same basis as the premature retirement example quoted above. The main reasons for the much improved saving compared with the granting of premature retirement to a 55 year old are that in this case, 25 years' salary payment is being saved instead of 10 years' and no pension is paid to the teacher between the date of leaving and the date of normal retirement. Of course, the "saving" depends on the critical assumption that the teacher would not decide to leave voluntarily; and it will be important (as well as difficult) to ensure that the better teachers do not take up the offer leaving those who are unable to find alternative employment.

**DELEGATING RESPONSIBILITY TO THE LOCAL LEVEL**

75. In its earlier report, *Obtaining Better Value in Education: Aspects of Non-Teaching Costs in Secondary Schools,* the Commission set out its reasons for believing that increased delegation of authority and responsibility to the school level is desirable. As that report stated (paragraphs 127 and 128): "the Commission considers that more delegation of authority and responsibility to the local level will result in better value for money and avoidance of waste, provided (the proviso is crucial) that the ground is properly prepared in advance". In theory, subject only to the requirements of the Education Acts, the constraints of an annual budget and nationally agreed terms and conditions of service, and to the curriculum agreed with the governors and the LEA there may be no limit to the authority of a head to shift resources as seems appropriate to provide the best service to pupils with the funds available. Some academic departments could be streng-

thened at the expense of others; non-teaching staff could be increased or reduced; expenditure on books, equipment and maintenance could be "paid for" by avoiding use of supply teachers, for example. And so forth.

76. The earlier report observed that recent experience with the MSC Technical and Vocational Education Initiative (TVEI) suggested that when head teachers are given a relatively unconstrained choice over the balance between teaching staff, non-teaching staff or materials, they welcome what is a possibility of extensive virement (that is, transferring expenditure from one budget head to another). The report suggested that the most obvious addition to most capitation schemes will be to give head teachers authority over items such as telephone costs, at least some of the funds for in-service training of teachers, examination fees and expenses (where schools have reason for discretion over examination entries) and control over books, materials and supplies. This control would include the possibility of transferring expenditure between budget headings and the facility to carry forward items from year to year. In addition to relatively small items of expenditure, there are three areas where giving heads increased authority and responsibility could be expected to bring benefits: heating and lighting costs, cleaning and maintenance.

77. The Commission also set out the requirements for increasing delegation successfully:
   (a) The strategy for change should be gradual and confined to selected schools in the first instance, with progress being carefully monitored.
   (b) The central organisation structure within the local education service must be adjusted to allow delegation – so that heads and governors are able to "make their own mistakes".
   (c) Accurate and timely management information needs to be available if overall financial control is not to be lost. The proposal in the 1986 *Education Bill* that LEAs should have a duty to give governors expenditure statements for their schools will make sure that each school has a basis of information. Provision of full requirements for management information will probably involve extensive use of new information technology with remote terminals linked to the central financial information system.
   (d) Staff support and management training should be made available to head teachers in those schools to be given additional delegated powers.

Establishing a scheme of delegation can be a long-term process taking perhaps five to seven years. However it is encouraging to note from auditors' reports that a number of LEAs are taking steps to delegate more authority and responsibility to local schools,

78. Careful preparation is essential if an LEA is to succeed in promoting increased delegation. Local authorities would be well-advised to consult those like Cambridgeshire and Solihull who have already pursued initiatives. The preparation must include the establishment of management systems which inform the authority about what happens within schools. But the main requirement is to ensure that head teachers and governors are competent to manage the resources allocated to them. This in turn requires:
   (i) Greater attention to the selection of head teachers of secondary schools.
   (ii) Management training for teachers intending to become head teachers in due course.

These twin requirements are discussed in detail below.

**Selecting head teachers**

79. The military maxim that "there are no bad troops, just bad officers" can be expected to apply to secondary schools as it does to businesses. The way that a school is managed by its head teacher and governors is perhaps the single most powerful influence on the nature and quality of the education it provides. It follows therefore that LEAs and governing bodies should devote very considerable time and resources to selecting head teachers – who might well be responsible for some £20 million (at current prices) of public expenditure during their tenure as heads.

80. Astonishingly, however, the selection of head teachers can only be described as in general need of urgent improvement; in some cases it is evidently a shambles. The report of a research project by the Open University, *The Selection of Secondary Head Teachers**, makes very disturbing reading.

- Candidates are not, for the most part, technically assessed: rather the selection of head teachers is carried out in an arbitrary and amateur way.
- Even LEA officers have relatively little knowledge of selection techniques and lack training in the full range of these. Interviews occupy a central part in the procedures, yet few instances of the practice of generally accepted good interview principles were observed.
- There was a marked absence of peer group assessment – the use of experienced head teachers to comment on the suitability of candidates. Appraisal systems for senior school staff were generally absent, yet these are needed for references to be reliable and relevant.
- The criteria against which candidates were being assessed remained implicit and unstated and varied both between the different selectors and different elimination stages. This was scarcely surprising because there was a general absence both of job descriptions and of specifications of the competences required to perform the job.
- As a result, there was general predominance of political conflict between the various selector groups [members of the LEA, governors, education officers] and the power of patronage appeared considerable.
- The final interviews were usually unstructured and final decisions were often made on an inappropriate basis. A range of random factors was employed as selection and eliminating criteria and among these "image stereotypes" tended to predominate, e.g. "a good disciplinarian", "classic Oxbridge type". Arriving at the appointment decisions at final interviews was unsystematic, rushed and often chaotic.

81. These observed weaknesses are very serious, given the importance of head teacher appointments to the quality of the secondary education system. The same report put forward some entirely sensible proposals for improving the selection process which the Commission believes should be acted upon:

(i) Candidates should be eliminated on the basis of their formal, systematic assessment in relation to factors related to their ability to carry out the responsibilities of head teachers. All candidates, internal and external, should be assessed according to the same criteria and using the same methods.

---

* ISBN 0 335 10410 X, Open University Press, 1983

(ii) Evidence on candidates should be recorded in writing and accumu-lated through each stage of the selection process; this contrasts with the present system where candidates usually start afresh, with a clean slate and equal chance after each elimination hurdle.

(iii) Candidates should be given an opportunity to visit the school before preliminary interviews and have adequate time there to absorb everything they feel they need to know. This part of the procedure should *not* constitute a component of the assessment procedure; neither should social functions be used to assess candidates.

(iv) All selectors present at the final interviews should receive a prior briefing, on the format of the interviews, each candidate's perform-ance so far, the allocation and ordering of questions, the mode of the assessment to be used and the mechanisms for arriving at the final decision. Questioning should be allocated according to selector expertise and interests.

(v) Officers responsible for secondary head teacher selection should be trained in selection. They should then organise the briefing and training of the members who will be involved. Seminars and specially prepared materials could include the following: the nature of the job, the competences to be sought, the procedures by which those competences are to be evaluated, interview techniques and methods for treating evidence and reaching a final decision.

(vi) Finally, the respective roles of education officers, members of the LEA and governors need to be clearly defined. The composition of the appointments committee should be a local matter. One possibility is that each LEA should maintain a head teacher appointment committee which would hold fixed diary dates open to allow for discussion of headship policy and the execution of selection procedures without the difficulties arising from having to compete for priority with other local government demands. The chairman of the appointment committee would be a member of the education authority, not least because "the need to appoint a new head arises infrequently in any particular school, but the local education authorities' concern with all schools in the area gives them considerable experience".* Governors should be represented in the selection procedure from the beginning; and the school governing body should nominate its selectors prior to the advertise-ment of the post and commencement of the selection procedure. The LEA officer responsible for the appointments of head teachers should be responsible for assembling all the relevant evidence and presenting it to the committee for decision. Specifically, it should be his or her duty to:

- lead the systematic determination of the job criteria, providing an explicit definition of the job and the schools required to carry it out;
- use appropriate means to secure evidence on the extent to which the various candidates are competent in the necessary areas;
- assemble and accumulate the evidence of candidates' strengths and weaknesses in the various school requirements in the form of complete profiles which can be used by members and governors for their final decision.

---

* *A New Partnership for our Schools,* Report of the Committee of Enquiry into the Management of Government of Schools, 1977.

**Management Training**

82. There has been a great deal of recent work in the field of management training, notably by the National Development Centre for School Management Training. This is just as well, given that head teachers previously had little formal management training even though they may well be stewards of capital assets worth some £600,000 at replacement cost and have a staff of approaching 100 people with an annual revenue budget of perhaps as much as £800,000. Until they become deputy heads, most teachers are not likely to have had any management training at all; and as deputy heads, they will generally be expected to learn by observation – as the present head did before them.

83. This is clearly a most unsatisfactory state of affairs. The Commission considers that management courses for aspiring head teachers should be developed – perhaps by the Open University and selected FE colleges. Once the courses are available and approved, no teacher should be considered for an appointment as deputy head unless and until he or she has attended the appropriate middle management course – exactly as is the case with officers in the Armed Forces, who must have been to a staff college if they wish to be considered for higher command. In the light of the availability now of suitable courses, once a new head teacher is appointed, he or she could go on a refresher course before taking up the appointment.

**INCREASING IN-SERVICE TRAINING**

84. Any well managed concern would expect to provide around 10 days off-the-job training to every staff member every year. In a people-intensive activity like teaching, the annual investment should be even greater than this – especially since the new initiatives (e.g. GCSE, TVEI, performance appraisal) mean that many teachers will need to acquire new skills. Moreover, there are serious shortages of teachers in mathematics, the sciences and technical/craft subjects: recent estimates suggest a shortage of 4,000 mathematics graduates in teaching and 1,600 physics graduates; and in 1985 the intakes to post-graduate secondary teacher training of graduates in these subjects were 856 and 273 respectively. So long as the recruitment shortfall continues, the gap will need to be closed as far as possible by in-service training including, particularly, retraining in new subject special-isms through one year full-time courses.

85. The question of the match between teachers' qualifications and what they are required to teach has received a good deal of attention in recent years. It has been argued to be a crucial determinant of teaching quality. In its latest expenditure report, HMI argue that:

"Poor match between teachers' initial qualifications and experience and what they were being called upon to do affected the quality of work in just over one-eighth of the lessons seen."

Table 10 shows that the extent of the mismatch in school staffing as defined by HMI is decreasing. The information comes from DES surveys.

Partly as a result of the perceived ill effects of mismatch the Government intends to amend the *Education (Teachers) Regulations 1982*, to require LEAs and the governors of aided schools to have regard to the formal qualifications of teachers in considering their fitness for appointment.

86. The study team has examined the question of match in a sample of 70 schools in 12 LEAs by asking heads to identify areas in which they felt teaching was rendered less effective by reason of match. They were asked to use a criterion of effectiveness such that a teacher who was not qualified or experienced in a particular subject but who was, in the view of the head, nonetheless teaching that subject successfully, would not be recorded as mismatched. The result of this investigation was that only around 1 per cent periods of mismatch in timetables established at September 1984 were identified. These results suggest that head teachers did not consider

*Table 10:* TEACHING AND TUITION PROVIDED BY SUBJECT OF QUALIFICATION

| | % Teachers teaching a subject for which they had no qualification | | % Tuition in a subject provided by teachers with no qualification | |
|---|---|---|---|---|
| | 1977 | 1984 | 1977 | 1984 |
| English | 30% | 29 | 17% | 14 |
| Physical education | 48 | 43 | 13 | 14 |
| Mathematics | 29 | 26 | 15 | 13 |
| History | 22 | 24 | 8 | 8 |
| Geography | 23 | 22 | 9 | 7 |
| Religious education | 59 | 58 | 29 | 24 |
| Art/light craft | 26 | 26 | 10 | 6 |
| French | 16 | 19 | 9 | 8 |
| Biology | 16 | 17 | 9 | 9 |
| Physics | 33 | 30 | 22 | 18 |
| Chemistry | 21 | 20 | 10 | 9 |
| Music | 23 | 25 | 6 | 6 |
| Craft, design and technology | N/A | N/A | 15 | 13 |
| Home economics | N/A | N/A | 6 | 6 |

Source: DES supplied data

mismatch to be a very significant factor in the provision of effective teaching at the outset of the year.

87. In addition to the views expressed in the questionnaire, there are other reasons for believing that national concern about mismatch may be misplaced:

(a) The definition of match is difficult. Many head teachers and education officers interviewed during this study maintained that lack of formal qualification does not necessarily mean that a teacher cannot adequately teach a lesson. Some weight should be given to experience and in-service training, and a more formal subject requirement may lead to inflexibility. This is especially so given rapid changes in the curriculum.

(b) The problem of match is partly one of shortage. Considering formal qualifications will not create more mathematics teachers.

Therefore, amendment of the *Education (Teachers) Regulations 1982* to require that LEAs and governors should have regard to formal qualifications when considering fitness of appointment does not seem particularly relevant to the problem of mismatch – indeed it could lead to unnecessary unfilled vacancies if undue weight is given to formal qualifications. Rather, the shortage of specialist subject teachers should be tackled directly in the ways described in the next chapter – notably by differential pay – and by retraining of teachers from other specialisms.

88. Against this background, the amount of in-service training provided for most teachers is inadequate. Expenditure per teacher averages around £50 a year (excluding salary costs of the trainee); this compares with expenditure on out-of-pocket costs of around £800 a year per staff member in the Commission which aims to provide every member of its staff with around 10 days off-the-job training a year. Moreover, the funds available for in-service training within an authority fluctuate sharply from year to year; and since teachers' staff complements are generally protected, training provision has to bear a disproportionate share of the reduction. Certainly, it seems that little attempt is generally made to relate the provision of funds to identified training needs. None of the LEAs visited by the study team provide any reliable information on the amount of in-service training made available for individual teachers before the recent industrial dispute. This was scarcely surprising. Table 11 (overleaf) based on responses to the Commission's questionnaire to chief education officers suggests that many LEAs lack some of the basic information needed to plan recruitment and training programmes:

*Table 11:* AVAILABILITY OF BASIC MANPOWER INFORMATION
% LEAs with information available at HQ (n = 34)

| | On-line | Within 2 days | Within 2 weeks | Not available |
|---|---|---|---|---|
| Staffing in each school | | | | |
| – grades | 68% | 20 | 6 | 6 |
| – subject qualifications | 44 | 32 | 18 | 6 |
| Individual in-service training records | 12 | 35 | 21 | 32 |
| Projections of natural wastage, by | | | | |
| – school | 18 | 15 | 38 | 29 |
| – subject specialisms | 9 | 24 | 41 | 26 |

89. However, it seems likely that even before the last 12 months, a typical teacher might receive no more than one or two days in-service training a year. Moreover, the in-service training which teachers do receive is often ill-focused and inadequately related to the needs of the education service:

- The providers of in-service training are many – universities, colleges of education, LEAs themselves and individual schools amongst others. These providers vary in the degree to which what they offer is influenced by the identified needs of LEAs and schools.
- The take-up of provision is haphazard, since it is in large part dependent on the willingness of individual teachers to volunteer the time required (and some of the money).

90. Following the White Paper, *Better Schools,* the government (with authority proposed in the 1986 *Education Bill*) is introducing a training grants scheme which requires that LEAs submit bids for funds for in-service training, both for the national priority areas and for areas which they have identified locally. Grants are then distributed to LEAs according to central assessments of the programmes outlined in the bids. This approach has begun to be put into effect with the introduction, through the MSC, of TVEI-related in-service training (TRIST).

91. While there is undoubtedly a need for more in-service training the value of a process of local bids for a share of national funds is questionable if it means that soundly based in-service training programmes do not go ahead. Every LEA needs in-service training funds, regardless of whether an officer can be found to write an impressive submission to the centre within a tight deadline. A more effective means of ensuring that the funds are well used would be a continuing central assessment of the in-service training actually carried out in each LEA, probably involving HMI.

92. Whatever means of funding is used for in-service training, individual schools will need some scope to initiate training to meet needs which heads and senior staff identify. In too many schools visited during the Commission's study, heads reported that teachers returning from courses were unable to make full use of the training which they had received. This was because the school (as opposed to the individual teacher) had no commitment to the course. Moreover, time is as essential to effective training as funding. Time for in-service training could most effectively be provided by including in teachers' conditions of service a requirement that the teachers' working year should be longer than pupils', by say ten days. Another potential source of time, at least for some teachers, is the period at the end of the summer term when examinations are over and examination groups are not taught. Since other pupils are being taught during this period, the time available is not in large blocks; any training done might therefore take the form of guided private study. That part of in-service training and related work which needs to be carried out during the school

day could be allowed for among the non-teaching elements of an ALS model.

*   *   *

The steps suggested above can in the main be tackled directly by LEAs. During the audit round for 1986–87, auditors will be pursuing these matters with them. However, experience over the past four to five years suggests that the prospects for action will be improved materially if steps are taken on a broader front. These are the subject of the next chapter of this report.

Exhibit 15

## LEA RESPONSE TO FALLING ROLLS

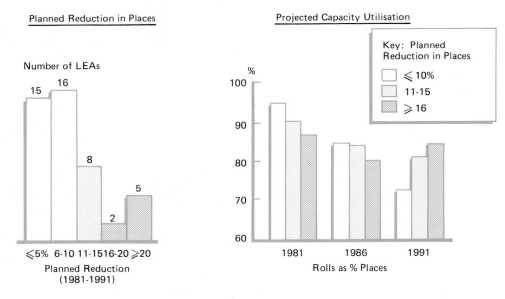

Planned Reduction in Places

Number of LEAs

Projected Capacity Utilisation

Key: Planned
Reduction in Places
⩽ 10%
11-15
⩾ 16

Planned Reduction
(1981-1991)

Rolls as % Places

Source: Audit Commission analysis of Auditors'reports, 1986

48

# 2  Making the Changes Possible

93. The previous chapter of this report has outlined steps that could be taken by LEAs and schools to improve secondary education within the existing legislative and organisational constraints. However, none of these steps is new and many have been taken by some authorities – suggesting that the current constraints can be overcome.

94. But the performance of the educational system as a whole over the past four to five years in adapting to falling secondary school rolls can only be described as poor. As described earlier, spare capacity has increased since 1981 and the outlook is for the situation to worsen over the next five years as rolls fall by a further 17–20 per cent in many areas.

- In a sample of 46 LEAs with a combined secondary school roll (in 1986) of over 1.8 million pupils (around half of the total) spare capacity rose from 8 per cent in 1981 to 16 per cent in 1986 and, on present plans, it will reach 25 per cent by 1991. On a national scale, this would mean by 1991 there will be over 800,000 empty places or the equivalent of more than 1,000 completely empty schools even after current plans have been implemented.
- The situation is probably more serious than these figures suggest, since the sample contains a disproportionate number of LEAs known to be taking active steps to deal with the problem. DES-endorsed targets for removing (only) 60 per cent of surplus places imply the equivalent of 200 – 250 closures a year for the period 1986–1992; but the average closure rate over the past five years was around 60 – indicating a cumulative shortfall by the end of 1991 against modest targets equivalent to at least 800 – 900 schools.
- Moreover, where capacity has been reduced, this has often been achieved by removing temporary accommodation rather than reorganising local secondary provision. In the five years to the end of 1985 the ratio of the removal of temporary and permanent places was close to 1:1. This yields fewer educational and financial benefits. In any case, since temporary accommodation accounts for less than 10 per cent of capacity in most LEAs, continued use of this "soft" option to reduce capacity will not be possible.

95. Exhibit 15 (opposite) shows that two thirds of the sample LEAs plan to reduce the number of places by 10 per cent or less between 1981 and 1991; only a small minority – less than one in five – is planning to manage the decline in rolls to avoid a further increase in spare capacity over the next five years. In short, a massive opportunity is being missed and with it the chance to improve the quality of secondary education and teachers' rewards for ability and effort without a large (£5–700 million a year) increase in taxation either directly or in the form of rate rises.

96. This disappointing performance over the past four to five years has convinced the Commission that the prospects for action along the lines recommended in Chapter One are poor and will remain poor unless there

are fairly radical changes in the framework within which the education service is managed. Specifically:

    (a) The arrangements for securing agreement to school reorganisations that have been laid down in legislation and the recent changes in the role and composition of governing bodies could have been designed to slow, if not prevent, the necessary closures taking place.

    (b) Local accountability is lacking. The Commission agrees with government's view as stated in a recent Green Paper, *Paying for Local Government,* that effective local accountability is the key to securing economy, efficiency and effectiveness in authorities' use of resources. But, so long as DES plays such a central role in the negotiations over pay and local reorganisation schemes on the one hand and confers additional powers on governing bodies on the other, it is difficult to see how an LEA can be held accountable for the quality of the local education service.

    (c) The present systems for controlling LEAs' revenue and capital expenditure make it difficult – if not impossible – to carry through many reorganisation proposals.

    (d) Teachers have little direct personal stake in promoting the reorganisation of local secondary schools, because there is insufficient local flexibility to determine pay and conditions of service.

    (e) The current machinery for negotiating teachers' pay and conditions is grotesquely inadequate to the needs of the education service.

97. These problems must be solved if the necessary reorganisation of secondary education is to be possible. Exhibit 16 shows the inter-relationships of the various problems and suggests how they combine to frustrate the kind of changes proposed in Chapter One. As a result, the short-term interests of local members of LEAs, school governors, teachers' representatives and Members of Parliament and Ministers combine to prevent – or at minimum delay – school closures for two to three years: it is almost invariably easier politically to sacrifice the quality of local education in the future in favour of avoiding the short-term political problems that closures inevitably bring in their wake. But unless schools are closed on a substantial scale – and soon – the opportunity to re-equip the service and to

Exhibit 16

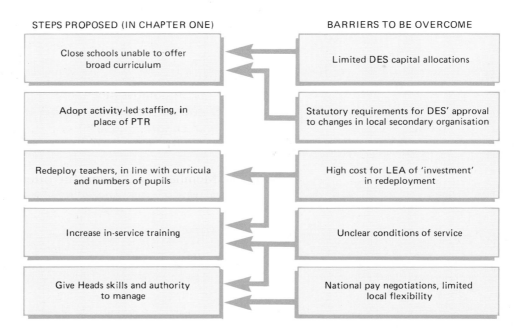

| STEPS PROPOSED (IN CHAPTER ONE) | BARRIERS TO BE OVERCOME |
|---|---|
| Close schools unable to offer broad curriculum | Limited DES capital allocations |
| Adopt activity-led staffing, in place of PTR | Statutory requirements for DES' approval to changes in local secondary organisation |
| Redeploy teachers, in line with curricula and numbers of pupils | High cost for LEA of 'investment' in redeployment |
| Increase in-service training | Unclear conditions of service |
| Give Heads skills and authority to manage | National pay negotiations, limited local flexibility |

improve the relative pay of its teachers will be forgone. Table 12 illustrates the scale of the problem – and of the opportunity.

Table 12: COST IMPLICATIONS OF DIFFERENT LEVELS OF SCHOOL REORGANISATION, 1991
Savings from falling rolls and closures in the period 1984–91, at 1986 prices

|  | £m | £/teacher |
|---|---|---|
| Assuming 1985 closure rate maintained | £135–150m | 700 |
| 'Minimum' closures | 450 | 2,400 |
| 'Maximum' closures | 710 | 3,900 |

The minimum and maximum closures are derived from the paper referred to in paragraph 15.

98. In the Commission's view, in addition to the changes proposed in Chapter One, measures need to be taken urgently to:

(i) Improve the prospects for securing local agreement to school reorganisation proposals.

(ii) Change the systems for controlling LEAs' revenue and capital expenditure, to enable the necessary investments in buildings and equipment and early retirement of teachers to be made; at the same time, the systems need to provide a greater incentive for authorities and local communities to make the painful choices involved.

(iii) Change the machinery for negotiating pay and conditions at the national level.

(iv) Introduce more local flexibility into the way teachers are managed.

The rest of this chapter describes the need for each of these steps in turn. In all cases, legislation will be needed to correct the present problems.

**IMPROVING THE PROSPECTS FOR SECURING LOCAL AGREEMENT TO SCHOOL CLOSURES**

99. The process for deciding the closure of secondary schools is a long and complex one. Implementation may well take two years after the final decision. The process is laid down in considerable detail in the *Education Act* of 1980. The potential obstacles to any reorganisation scheme are clearly formidable:

– The chances of securing agreement from the local education committee are poor, particularly when the committee decides issues on narrow political lines and includes teachers' representatives.

– Almost any school can rely on being able to generate support for a campaign against its closure from at least 10 parents of present pupils who are also electors – even if (as is most unlikely) the governors themselves agree to the LEA's proposals; so formal objections are almost inevitable.

– Parents' concerns are most unlikely to be allayed by reassurance from their childrens' teachers, particularly in present circumstances. So the inevitable opposition becomes more strident, fuelled by teachers' opposition.

– Local Members of Parliament often become involved: school closures are a very emotional local issue and they provide a useful means for the Member to demonstrate that he has some "clout" with Ministers.

– Finally, all proposals may by law be reviewed by the Secretary of State and many must be reviewed by him. During the six year period 1980–85, some 86 per cent of closure proposals have in fact been reviewed by him. This acts as a deterrent to LEAs putting forward closure proposals. At minimum, there will be delay of up to a year while the proposals are considered in London, dragging out the local political problems. At worst, the proposals could be turned down, causing very considerable local political embarrassment.

In short, all the pressures are against radical change in the local secondary education system; and protest costs the protester nothing. In these circumstances, it is scarcely surprising that the interests of future pupils and of those who are paying for the service often receive scant consideration when plans are made for the future.

100. The situation is complicated further by the existence of voluntary schools. Of the 4,444 secondary schools maintained by LEAs in England, 880 are voluntary aided, controlled or special agreement schools. Most of these are religiously based. The details of the status of these schools are complicated but, in addition to problems of redeployment mentioned below, the special status of these schools gives rise to difficulties for an LEA to include them in its reorganisation proposals. These difficulties would be compounded by one of the stipulations in the 1986 *Education Bill*, which would require that once the governing body of an aided school has decided at a meeting to serve notice of discontinuance of the school, the decision should not take effect until confirmed at a second meeting 28 or more days after the first.

101. The 1944 *Education Act* stipulates that the contract of employment of a teacher in a voluntary aided school is with the governing body of the school, a body on which the religious or other representatives are in the majority (this does not apply to voluntary controlled schools, which are less common at secondary level); but the salary of a teacher in a voluntary aided school is paid by the LEA maintaining the school. This apportionment of power and responsibility between the LEA and the governors inhibits the LEA's management of the teaching force. In particular, the scope for redeployment of teachers from schools where rolls have fallen is reduced. If the intended receiving school for a redeployed teacher is a voluntary aided one, the governors have the power to block the redeployment, either because the nominated individual does not hold religious views approved by the governors or simply because the governors hope to appoint a teacher better suited to the post from public advertisement. Voluntary schools thus further complicate the problem of managing falling rolls – particularly since, as Table 13 shows, they tend to be smaller than county schools – although the effect of parental choice over the past 5 years has offset falling school rolls.

*Table 13:* AVERAGE SIZE OF SECONDARY SCHOOLS
England only (excluding middle deemed secondary)

|  | 1980 | 1984 | % Change |
|---|---|---|---|
| Voluntary schools |  |  |  |
| – Controlled | 825 | 858 | +4.0 |
| – Aided | 716 | 744 | +3.9 |
| – Special agreement | 720 | 709 | (1.5) |
| County schools | 927 | 925 | (0.2) |

102. The Commission has concluded that the following steps need to be considered to facilitate the process, illustrated in Exhibit 17 (opposite), of securing agreement to school closures:

Exhibit 17

**The process for reorganising secondary schools is long and complex**

THE REORGANISATION PROCESS IN
SECONDARY SCHOOLS — 1984

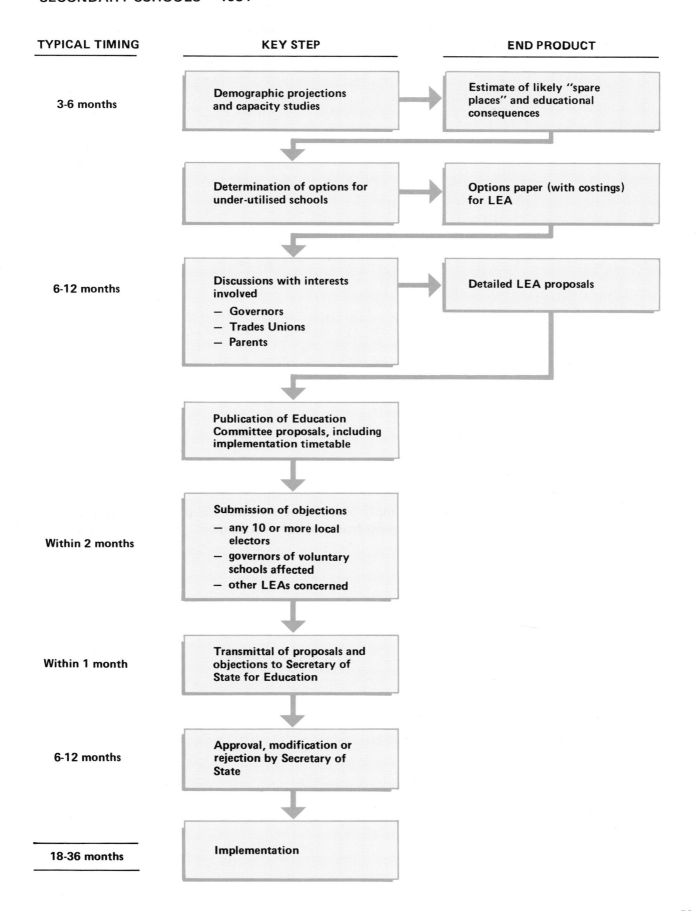

| TYPICAL TIMING | KEY STEP | END PRODUCT |
|---|---|---|
| 3-6 months | Demographic projections and capacity studies | Estimate of likely "spare places" and educational consequences |
| | Determination of options for under-utilised schools | Options paper (with costings) for LEA |
| 6-12 months | Discussions with interests involved<br>— Governors<br>— Trades Unions<br>— Parents | Detailed LEA proposals |
| | Publication of Education Committee proposals, including implementation timetable | |
| Within 2 months | Submission of objections<br>— any 10 or more local electors<br>— governors of voluntary schools affected<br>— other LEAs concerned | |
| Within 1 month | Transmittal of proposals and objections to Secretary of State for Education | |
| 6-12 months | Approval, modification or rejection by Secretary of State | |
| 18-36 months | Implementation | |

(i)    Membership of local education committees should be streamlined, so that not more than (say) one-third of the members of the parent authority sit on the education committee. It will be difficult enough securing agreement of the education committee to painful decisions; the situation will be even worse if, as is not unknown, the education committee comprises the entire parent authority of perhaps 80 – 90 members. In addition, the presence of teacher representatives on education committees is questionable: they will invariably have a vested interest in most of the decisions made; and it should be for the education officers to provide the necessary professional input to the committee deliberations.

(ii)   The confidence of members of LEAs in putting forward closure proposals would be increased if they had a clearer understanding of the criteria that the Secretary of State will apply in considering reorganisation schemes. The Commission has been assured by DES officials that a set of clear and explicit criteria exists and that they are always willing to discuss individual cases informally. However, the Commission notes that these assurances come as something of a surprise to many of the LEAs consulted in the course of the study. Publication of the criteria should speed up the process of evaluating reorganisation schemes; the Commission would like to see all proposals decided within four months and, perhaps, deemed to be approved if the DES has not responded within that time with the kind of statement of reasons that an auditor is required to give when announcing his decisions on objections to authorities' accounts.

(iii)  Delays in securing the Secretary of State's approval would be reduced if he did not have to approve all reorganisation schemes involving objection or voluntary schools. If the objection requirements were changed the objection process could be made less easy, e.g. by requiring (say) 750 local electors to object to a reorganisation scheme. This would mean that it would usually be necessary for the objectors to secure the support of people other than the present parents of pupils at the school facing closure. The Secretary of State could simply "call in" re-organisation proposals – as happens with planning applications now – which have aroused particularly stiff local opposition, presumably for good reasons. At present, some 14 per cent of proposals for reorganisation already go through automatically, because no formal local objection is made and the Secretary of State has not given notice of his intention to require approval.

(iv)   More inducements could be made available to a local community to accept closures. It might help if the educational disbenefits of small group sizes were more apparent to parents: as one LEA member put it "the most powerful incentive [to agreeing to closure proposals] would be the realisation that unless it went ahead, the quality of their child's education was certain to suffer. At present, parents with children at small schools are simply not convinced of the educational arguments. Perhaps HMI could help us?" At the same time, in view of the urgency of the situation, there might be a case for a specific secondary school reorganisation grant (of £x per place) to encourage the acceptance of change.

(v)    Except for teachers of religious education as a main subject in voluntary aided schools, redeployment of teachers into and out of all secondary schools should be controlled by LEAs, with head teachers and governors being consulted.

(vi) Finally, local accountability would be strengthened if the additional costs incurred as a result of local opposition to closure proposals could be made to fall on the community directly responsible. At present, the opportunity cost of protest is small, which can encourage an irresponsible attitude among the special interests concerned. If some at least of the additional costs fell directly on the neighbours of those protesting against a local closure, minds might be concentrated more tightly on the merits of the case. But the Commission recognises the practical difficulties of identifying who should bear the costs and how they might be imposed.

## CHANGING THE EXPENDITURE CONTROL SYSTEMS

103. The rate support grant, paid by the taxpayer, includes an allowance for secondary education equal to around half the annual cost (but there are wide variations in the amounts reaching the education service in different authorities). The Commission has already drawn attention to the serious weaknesses in the present systems for distributing the grant among local authorities and in the mechanisms by which Government now seeks to control (separately) authorities' gross revenue and capital expenditure. There is no point in rehearsing the evidence here – not least because the weaknesses are now widely accepted. The recent Green Paper, *Paying for Local Government*, represents an attempt to correct a clearly unsatisfactory situation, and the Commission will be publishing its detailed views on these latest proposals in due course.

104. However, there are two respects in which the present systems stand in the way of the radical reorganisation of secondary education which the present situation demands:

(i) The most recent change in the grant distribution machinery has made it more expensive for authorities facing the greatest fall in school rolls to invest in reorganisation; and, at the extreme, rate capping may prevent some authorities from taking the very steps suggested earlier.

(ii) The system for controlling capital expenditure limits the incentive for authorities to sell off under-utilised land and buildings; and, again at the extreme, it may prevent authorities from undertaking the capital works needed to reorganise the local schools – estimated at some £1,250 – £1,500 per place.

Each of these problems is discussed in more detail below.

## Adverse effect of recent changes in grant distribution

105. The arrangements for distributing rate support grant to local authorities change regularly – the uncertainty that these changes induce is itself an important cause of waste and is a stimulant to creative accounting as well as to delays in submitting accounts for audit. [Six months after the end of the last financial year 1984–85, 19 education authorities had not presented their accounts to the external auditor].

106. The most recent change has been to shift the basis on which grant is paid to authorities from the Government's expenditure targets to the grant related expenditure (GRE). The Commission will be commenting separately on the merits of the change. However, in the present context, the effect is that the cost of secondary school reorganisations remains higher than it needs to be in many of those authorities facing the most difficult problems. This is because:

(a) The fall in school rolls tends to be greatest in the more deprived authorities, where the total population has declined most markedly. The problem is particularly serious in London as the following

percentage changes in secondary school population for the period
1981–86 show:

| | |
|---|---|
| Inner London | −24.2% |
| Outer London | −16.4 |
| Metropolitan districts | −12.0 |
| Shire counties, England | − 9.2 |
| Wales | − 8.1 |

(b) As total expenditure increases above GRE, the amount of grant receivable declines. As a result, every extra £100 spent costs the local authority considerably more than this – up to £292 in the case of the London Boroughs of Hounslow, for instance. This is the way the present system is designed. Because of the recent shift, some "safety net" arrangements have been introduced; but these are by definition transitory.

(c) Unfortunately most inner city authorities have traditionally spent considerably above GRE. In 1984–85 metropolitan districts were spending some 3.5 per cent above GRE and London authorities (combined) 18 per cent above. By contrast shire counties were spending 3.4 per cent below GRE. The reason for the rather different spending pattern, according to the authorities concerned, is that the GRE assessment does not allow sufficiently for the compounding effects of the concentration of different problems in inner city areas.

107. The effect of the grant distribution arrangements is to increase the cost of investment in school reorganisation for virtually all LEAs; in some cases the cost to local ratepayers is as much as twice the original cash outlay. The following table illustrates the costs to a cross section of authorities of offering voluntary redundancy to 100 teachers at a cost of £20,000 per teacher that should therefore be costing £2 million. In fact, because of the vagaries of the grant system, the cost to the local ratepayers will range from £2.8 million to £5.8 million.

*Table 14:*   COST OF VOLUNTARY REDUNDANCY
100 teachers in selected authorities
£ million

| | £m |
|---|---|
| Shropshire | 2.8 |
| Liverpool | 2.9 |
| Hampshire | 3.2 |
| Cleveland | 3.5 |
| Manchester | 3.7 |
| Wolverhampton | 3.8 |
| Berkshire | 4.0 |
| Hounslow | 5.8 |
| [Base cost 100 × £20,000 | 2.0] |

It will be apparent that the present grant arrangements provide a disincentive for authorities to invest in secondary reorganisation.

\*       \*       \*

Faced with these problems, many LEAs have opted to capitalise redundancy costs. But in this area, too, the present control systems introduce a formidable range of obstacles.

**Constraints on capital spending**

108. The systems for controlling local authorities' capital expenditure could affect the prospect for securing local secondary school reorganisation in at least two ways: the authority may lack the authorisation for the necessary capital expenditure on new buildings and alterations; and the

incentive to press ahead may be reduced if the authority cannot apply the proceeds of the sale of surplus land and buildings to priority local developments. The present control systems combine these two potentially perverse influences.

109. Taking the second point first, at present LEAs may apply only 30 per cent of any receipts from selling school land and buildings to supplement their capital allocations made by the various government departments. The process is described in the Commission's earlier report on *Capital Expenditure Controls in Local Government in England* published just over a year ago*. The government's most recent consultation paper** on the system, issued in February 1986, promises little near-term relief. Paragraph 10 is scarcely reassuring, even after translation into English:

"Although receipts would not immediately constitute additional spending power, authorities would know that they would represent spending power [4 – 5 years] in the future, and so would still have an incentive to make such sales. The Government would as now be able to vary the proportion of spending power derived from receipts. On the information now available, the Government envisages that the spending power from a particular type of receipt over whatever averaging period was chosen would be at least as great as the power derived over the same period in the present system under the prescribed proportions of capital receipts set out in DOE Circular 17/85. Unless the proportion were set at 100 per cent in a particular case, the remainder of the receipt would be taken into account at national level in determining the total for the needs based

Exhibit 18

**CAPITAL EXPENDITURE ON SCHOOLS\* IN ENGLAND 1980-1989**
**£m, at 1985 prices**

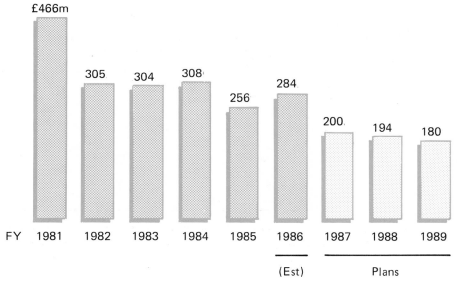

\* Primary and Secondary Schools

Source: Audit Commission analysis of
The Government's Expenditure Plans, 1985-86 to 1987-88 (Table 3.10)

\* ISBN 0 11 701280 7, HMSO, price £4.80 net
\*\* *Review of Local Authority Capital Expenditure Control Systems in England and Wales*, February 1986

element of allocations. *It would not be available at any time to the authority which generated the receipt to justify additional capital spending* [emphasis added], although the cash would of course be available to that authority to repay debt or to finance expenditure within allocations".

110. Lack of positive local incentives is clearly not going to be helpful in the present extraordinarily difficult situation facing LEAs seeking to close schools. In addition, there may simply not be sufficient allocations of capital spending. Exhibit 18 shows that there has been a steady decline in real terms in capital expenditure on primary and secondary schools since 1979; and as the Exhibit also shows, the decline is forecast to continue according to government's most recent expenditure plans. Estimates suggest that the total capital expenditure requirement entailed by the potential secondary school reorganisation programme could be of the order of £1.5 – 2 billion, including the maintenance backlog of some £6 – 700 million that has built up over the past decade. This compares with annual capital allocations projected for the next three years of under £250 million a year. Local investigations tend to confirm the capital shortfall. There is usually a substantial difference between the bids submitted by LEAs and (one year) capital allocations that they eventually receive from DES. Table 15 shows the situation for the ten authorities examined in the Commission's study of the present capital expenditure controls.

*Table 15:* CAPITAL EXPENDITURE ON EDUCATION, 1984–85
£m, Selected authorities

| Authority | Bid | Allocation | Discount |
|---|---|---|---|
| A | £1.7m | 0.8 | 53% |
| B | 2.7 | 1.0 | 63 |
| C | 1.8 | 1.2 | 33 |
| D | 3.7 | 3.3 | 11 |
| E | 3.8 | 1.7 | 55 |
| F | 2.0 | 2.0 | 0 |
| G | 7.5 | 3.6 | 52 |
| H | 10.4 | 6.5 | 47 |
| I | 2.8 | 1.4 | 50 |
| J | 7.5 | 5.0 | 33 |
| TOTAL | 43.9 | 26.5 | 40 |

Clearly, on this evidence it would be unwise to assume that planned capital allocations will be sufficient to support the likely capital costs of reorganising secondary education on the scale required.

111. This is not the place to go into the wider issues involved in the systems now in place and proposed for controlling local authorities' revenue and capital spending. However, the damage to the secondary school reorganisation effort caused by the present systems could be limited while a more satisfactory longer term solution is developed, by:

(i)   Ignoring payments designed to secure early retirement or voluntary severance when fixing rate support grant payments to LEAs. The effect would be that extra expenditure for the purpose of reducing numbers of teachers would not be penalised by a withdrawal of grant – although the full cost would, of course, still fall on the LEA in the first instance.

(ii)  Allowing LEAs to apply all capital receipts from the sale of school land and buildings to increased capital expenditure on local services, provided that the authority made clear that this was what it was doing. Clearly, the same receipt could not simultaneously be used both to fund increased expenditure and to retire debt – in effect being counted twice in the public sector borrowing requirement (PSBR) statistics.

112. The justification for these exceptions to the existing general rules is quite straightforward. The scale of the potential opportunities in secondary school reorganisation far outweighs any benefits that might be expected to flow from tighter control over the PSBR by penalising revenue expenditure on early retirement or voluntary severance compensation for teachers or limiting the incentive for LEAs to sell unwanted school land and buildings. Moreover, there need be no risk of the additional local authority expenditure "leaking" into other areas of spending.

**CHANGING THE MACHINERY FOR NEGOTIATING TEACHERS' PAY AND CONDITIONS**

113. There is clearly something seriously wrong with the way in which teachers' pay and conditions are determined. The difficulties in reaching a pay settlement for 1985 and the associated disagreements about conditions of service are but the most recent and damaging of a number of failures of the process. On teachers' pay alone there have been two major enquiries – the Houghton Committee and the Clegg Committee – and a number of cases of referral to arbitration. The record of inquiries and arbitrations on main pay since 1970 compares poorly with that of the other major negotiating bodies in local government:

| Manual Workers NJC | 2 |
| APT and C NJC | 3 |
| Burnham P & S | 8 |

Arbitration is a valuable element of good industrial relations practice; but the frequency of recourse to it indicates a failing in the processes which are used before arbitration.

114. Another failing is the restriction placed on the recognition of good teaching through higher pay. Higher pay is generally only available through the promotion process, and promotion usually (though not invariably) entails the addition of management responsibilities to a teacher's classroom teaching duties. In practice LEAs normally allow head teachers to promote teachers for any of a large number of reasons, though in some cases broad guidelines are given. Specific intervention from LEA advisers is common for new schools and for schools which are shrinking. Among the reasons for offering promoted posts to teachers on appointment and for offering promotion within the school are:

(a) The post contains a managerial element, e.g. head of faculty or head of department.
(b) It contains a broad element of pastoral work in addition to teaching, e.g. head of house, head of upper or lower school, head of year.
(c) It contains some "added duty" element, e.g. responsibility for timetabling, out-of-school activities, home-school liaison.
(d) Local market forces make recruitment on normal terms difficult for shortage subjects – it may be that the only way of obtaining or keeping a mathematics teacher is to award a higher scale post.
(e) As a reward for being a good class teacher.
(f) More dubious reasons – keeping an awkward member of staff quiet, obtaining the moral support of influential members of staff.

In interviewing some 74 head teachers, it became apparent to the study team that head teachers consider all reasons but the last to be perfectly valid and very much a matter for managerial and educational judgement within the school.

115. The question of promotion prospects is particularly important now that increasing numbers of teachers are reaching the top of the incremental scales for their grades; the fall in school rolls has led to a reduction in promotion opportunities for teachers as Table 16 indicates:

*Table 16:* TEACHERS AT THE TOP OF THEIR RESPECTIVE SCALES
% in post in January

| Grade | 1976 | 1978 | 1980 | 1982 |
|---|---|---|---|---|
| Scale 1 | 12.0 | 15.6 | 18.0 | 23.5 |
| Scale 2 | 26.8 | 35.8 | 40.3 | 47.6 |
| Scale 3 | 30.0 | 43.1 | 48.9 | 56.6 |
| Scale 4 | 48.5 | 62.7 | 68.8 | 77.5 |
| Senior teacher | 73.4 | 83.9 | 88.8 | 92.7 |

Exhibit 19 highlights the extent of the change in the last few years. The major problem is at Scales 2 and 3 which contain the large majority of teachers; and it is clear that authorities can no longer rely on the salary scales to motivate many teachers to produce superior performance when their local promotion prospects are limited. New approaches are needed.

Exhibit 19

**TEACHERS AT THE TOP OF THEIR RESPECTIVE SALARY SCALES, 1976 and 1982**

**% teachers in post**

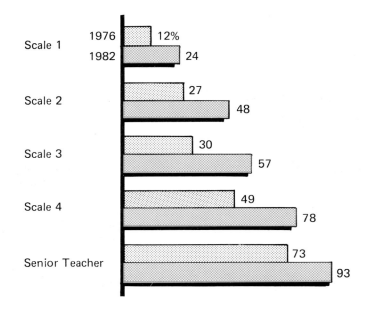

Source: Audit Commission analysis of LACSAB information, 1986

116. It will therefore come as no surprise to observers of the increasingly bitter industrial dispute that there is a serious problem in the pay structure for teachers. The evidence that major changes are in order is persuasive in the Commission's view:
  – Salaries of teachers in the United Kingdom are generally lower than those of comparable professions, as Exhibit 20 (showing interquartile ranges of gross earnings) demonstrates; and compared, for example, to the police, teachers in England and Wales are notably less well paid than their counterparts on the continent.

Exhibit 20

# PAY COMPARISONS FOR SELECTED OCCUPATIONS, 1984
## Range as % Survey Mean

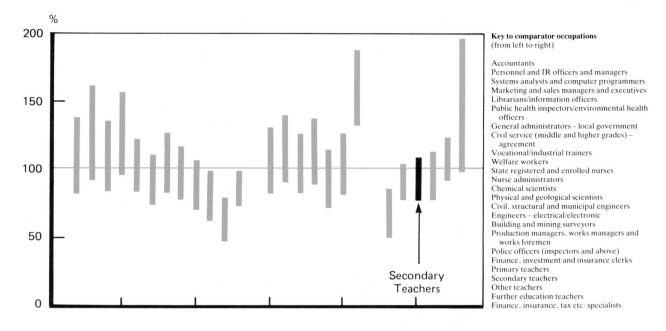

**Key to comparator occupations**
(from left to right)

Accountants
Personnel and IR officers and managers
Systems analysts and computer programmers
Marketing and sales managers and executives
Librarians/information officers
Public health inspectors/environmental health
    officers
General administrators – local government
Civil service (middle and higher grades) –
    agreement
Vocational/industrial trainers
Welfare workers
State registered and enrolled nurses
Nurse administrators
Chemical scientists
Physical and geological scientists
Civil, structural and municipal engineers
Engineers – electrical/electronic
Building and mining surveyors
Production managers, works managers and
    works foremen
Police officers (inspectors and above)
Finance, investment and insurance clerks
Primary teachers
Secondary teachers
Other teachers
Further education teachers
Finance, insurance, tax etc. specialists

Source: New Earnings Survey, 1984

# PAY OF EXPERIENCED MATHS TEACHERS*, 1985
## % Difference from Other Occupations

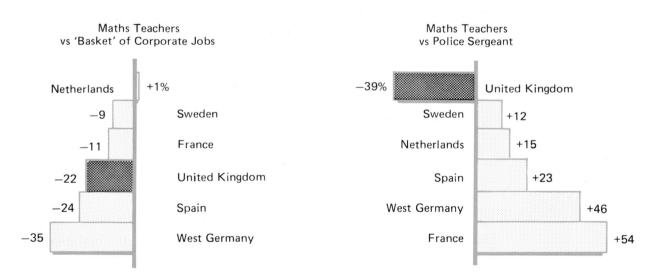

* In a Provincial town, with 5 years experience

Source: Audit Commission analysis of information provided by Hay-MSL, March 1986

- There is a serious shortage of teachers in particular subjects – notably mathematics and physics; the problem is particularly acute in certain geographic areas where the private sector is short of people with these particular skills.
- Teachers' classroom performance is not reflected in the pay structure, other than through promotion. This, too, is scarcely surprising since no agreed basis for assessing teachers' performance exists, still less a means of reflecting teaching performance in pay.
- Aspects of teachers' conditions of service that should be managed locally are causing considerable problems, most notably lunchtime supervision.

117. The Commission has concluded that solving these problems will require:

(i) Negotiation of pay and conditions of service together, rather than separately as at present.

(ii) Changes in the negotiating machinery itself; the Burnham arrangements have outlived their usefulness.

Each of these steps is discussed below.

**Simultaneous negotiation of pay and conditions of service**

118. Any sensible arrangement for employment makes clear what the employee is expected to do and what he or she will receive for doing it. Where the employer engages a large number of staff to undertake a particular class of duties, it is usually considered sensible that the duties and remuneration should be carefully defined for all to see. Where the duties involve a large element of discretion – as is the case in all professions – too precise a definition of duties constrains the exercise of professional expertise and is often counter-productive. The problem in such cases is to ensure that the employer knows what he is paying for while at the same time enabling the professional to exercise the full range of professional discretion. In the Commission's view:

(a) A teacher's professional discretion has to be relied upon whilst he or she is in class and teaching; and participation in the activities of school clubs and expeditions in school holidays should be left to teachers' professional commitment.

(b) Teaching duties outside class (e.g. course preparation, marking, staff meetings and liaison with parents) should be subject to some control, whether they are discharged during or outside the school day.

119. In the case of teachers, *Conditions of Service of Teachers in England and Wales* (the so-called Burgundy Book), summarises the various agreements reached since the 1944 *Education Act*. It refers to the Burnham document as the salary determinant, and makes no pronouncement on the definition of the teacher's day, duties or holiday entitlement – it says: "There are no existing national collective agreements on these matters beyond that affecting the school 'midday break'." In fact, although the Burgundy Book has its uses in dealing with the host of issues facing any employee of a large organisation, it can hardly be said to deal with the major questions of what a teacher should be doing and how he or she should be rewarded.

120. Perhaps the most serious weakness of the present arrangements is that they entail separate discussion of the inter-related issues of pay and conditions of service. Under the provisions of the *Remuneration of Teachers Act* of 1965 the Committee which considers the remuneration of school teachers (the Burnham Primary and Secondary Committee) deals solely with pay. There is no direct relationship with other conditions of service

which are negotiated directly between employers and teachers through a committee representing the Council of Local Education Authorities and school teacher associations (CLEA/ST).

121. This cannot be sensible; and the Commission urges that consideration be given to setting up machinery which permits pay and conditions of service to be discussed in the same forum. As far as is possible that machinery should be designed to be free of problems inherent in the current Burnham machinery that are discussed below.

**The Burnham machinery**

122. To put it as politely as possible, the present machinery for negotiating teachers' pay is cumbersome in the extreme. The *Remuneration of Teachers Act* requires the Secretary of State to establish one or more Burnham Committees to consider the remuneration of teachers, to appoint a chairman, nominate departmental representatives, determine which bodies shall represent LEAs and teachers on the committees (along with the number of representatives), and to specify which teachers are to have their remuneration reviewed. The Act requires each Burnham Committee to review pay when it thinks fit or when the Secretary of State directs. The Secretary of State is required to give effect to the recommendations statutorily by order which is then binding upon LEAs. There are also provisions in the Act on the conduct of arbitration, and in particular a provision for Parliament to reject recommendations of arbitration if national economic circumstances so require.

123. The Burnham Primary and Secondary Committee has 55 (sic) members, and consists of a management panel of 27 (including two DES representatives) and a teachers' panel of 28. A chairman is appointed by the Secretary of State. The composition of the panels is shown at Exhibit 21.

Exhibit 21

**COMPOSITION OF BURNHAM PANELS**

|  | NUMBER OF REPRESENTATIVES |
|---|---|
| **MANAGEMENT PANEL** | |
| Association of County Councils | 13 |
| Association of Metropolitan Authorities | 10 |
| Welsh Joint Education Committee | 2 |
| Department of Education and Science | 2 |
| | |
| **TEACHERS' PANEL** | |
| NUT | 13 |
| NAS/UWT | 7 |
| NAHT | 2 |
| AMMA | 4 |
| SHA | 1 |
| PAT | 1 |

The rules of procedure for the Primary and Secondary Committee as well as the FE Committee provide for each panel to express its joint view through one or more spokesmen. A verbatim record of the proceedings of the Burnham Committee is kept. Until July 1985, when it was repudiated by the local authority side, there was a Concordat with the Secretary of State which gave the two DES representatives 15 votes between them on the management panel (and the right of veto on any offer on grounds of cost) whilst every other representative had one vote. Furthermore, it prescribed that the management panel "will speak with one voice" and not disclose its proceedings to the public or to the teachers' panel.

124. It is inevitable that cumbersome negotiating machinery produces complex agreements based on the lowest common denominator of the various interests involved and allowing minimal local flexibility. The present problems over teachers' career structure are a case in point. Although Burnham Committees may review salaries when they think fit, in practice they do so each year and the Secretary of State publishes the outcome in, for the case of school teachers, *Scales of Salaries for Teachers: Primary and Secondary Education, England and Wales*. The document is very complex. Most teachers have only a passing knowledge of the content, and many LEAs recognise that one particular officer is the resident "expert" on it. The wording is obscure and reading of the text requires constant reference to other parts of it. Indeed, the complexity is such that in 1981 the management panel asked a group of officers and advisers to recommend how it could be simplified and made more responsive to educational needs. In past years, difficulties with the document have been so openly recognised that each year a commentary and set of guidance notes was published, first by the then Secretary of the Association of Education Committees and later by the joint secretaries of the Burnham Committee. The complexity results in differing interpretations of provisions between authorities; for example, the way that part-time teachers' pay is determined seems to vary.

125. The result bears all the hallmarks of the bureaucracy that produced it:

- It is complex. Since 1975 there have been four overlapping scales which cover the majority of teachers in ordinary schools. In addition to these Scales 1 to 4, there are scales for senior teachers, deputy head teachers and head teachers.
- It is mechanistic. A points system (summarised in Exhibit 22) determines how much head teachers and their deputies are paid as well as how many teachers can be appointed to Scales 2–4 and senior teacher posts within a particular school and therefore the local promotion possibilities available. In essence, the Burnham points allocation of a school is determined by a "unit total" calculated by assigning units to each pupil according to age and summing over all pupils in a school:
  - the unit total for a school determines the school's "group"
  - that group defines the salary scales on which the head teacher and deputy head teacher are paid
  - a published conversion table gives a "points score range" for schools falling in a given unit total range.
- It limits local flexibility. Only within the points score range do LEAs see themselves as having discretion to assign a points score to a particular school (theoretically there are rules allowing discretion to exceed the maximum; the majority of authorities exercise some, but not always maximum discretion).
- It involves uncertainty. The points entitlement of the school is

recalculated every three years, and is based on the average unit total for that year and the preceding two years. As rolls fall, authorities' unit totals and consequent points entitlements are declining rapidly.

Exhibit 22

**THE BURNHAM POINTS SYSTEM**

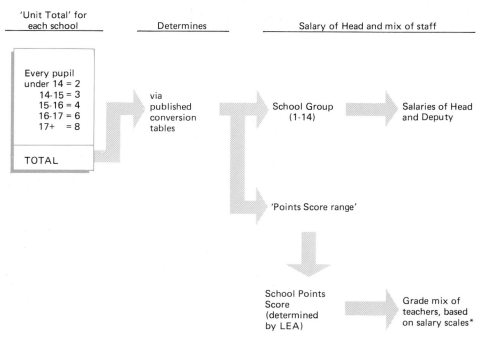

| 'Unit Total' for each school | Determines | Salary of Head and mix of staff |

Every pupil
under 14 = 2
14-15 = 3
15-16 = 4
16-17 = 6
17+ = 8

TOTAL

via published conversion tables

School Group (1-14)

Salaries of Head and Deputy

'Points Score range'

School Points Score (determined by LEA)

Grade mix of teachers, based on salary scales*

* Scale 1 = 0 points, Scale 2 = 1 point, etc.

126. Both the salary scale arrangements and the points system are at issue at present. Their reconsideration forms part of the question of the relationship between teachers' pay and conditions of service discussed above. However, one major management consideration emerges from the points system which highlights the connection with conditions of service, namely the question of whether teachers are paid to manage or to teach.

127. There is a need to reward good teaching since once in class, the teacher is the sole deliverer of education and guidance to the pupil. However, there is no doubt that a school cannot run without a managerial input; at the very least each department or faculty requires organisation of what it is to deliver and how. It is almost universally accepted that management requires status and that status depends on pay. The quandary is how to reward the best of non-managing teachers with the best possible salary whilst awarding managing teachers a salary which provides the status to manage. There is no simple answer, but the Commission believes that the question of separate recognition of professional teaching achievement and of managerial responsibility should figure large in any consideration of a major revision of the machinery for determining pay and conditions of service.

128. In the view of the Commission, this machinery should be changed because it does not provide an adequate vehicle for negotiation:

(a) The expression of a "joint view" through spokesmen for each panel along with the keeping of a verbatim record inhibits negotiation within the Committee itself. Anything other than "ritual" negotiation must take place outside the Committee, that is "behind the chair".

(b) The sheer size of each panel (there can be advisers as well as members present) means that even within individual panels the process of debate and decision-making is cumbersome and time-consuming; and the resulting agreements are inevitably rigid and complex.

(c) The influence of the Secretary of State (through the panel representing one of the parties to the negotiation) blurs public accountability for the quality of the education service: if the present terms are not sufficient to allow LEAs to attract and retain teachers of the necessary calibre in certain subjects, who should the public blame – the Secretary of State or the LEA facing local vacancies that it cannot fill?

\*     \*     \*

Whatever arrangements are eventually agreed between the interested parties, it will be essential that the resulting machinery is much smaller, does not involve the direct participation of the Secretary of State's representatives and, perhaps most important, leaves more room for local flexibility. This last requirement is discussed further below.

**PROVIDING MORE LOCAL FLEXIBILITY**

129. The Commission would like to see teachers able to benefit directly from the increases in productivity and the cost savings that will result from local school reorganisation. There is no doubt that many teachers' lives will be disrupted; and without the goodwill of the teachers, any reorganisation will be more difficult to "carry" through the local community and less effective once it has been implemented. This implies much more local flexibility in matters of pay and conditions of service than is now possible.

130. In addition to the problems discussed above, at least four personnel management issues are causing particular concern within the education service at present: the shortage of teachers for certain specialist subjects, assessement arrangements, ways of recognising teachers' performance through their pay, arrangements for controlling and responding to teacher absence, and arrangements for lunchtime supervisions. All are being discussed at the national level. Yet it is apparent that in each case the problems should be addressed locally and solutions appropriate to local traditions and market conditions developed within the framework agreed at the national level. Because each of these problems is important in its own right, they are discussed below with the Commission's rationale for a local rather than a national solution.

**Overcoming shortages of teachers**

131. A major difficulty in recruitment is the lack of applicants for teaching posts in particular specialisms, notably mathematics, physics and CDT. The problem is highlighted by the reduction in intakes in these subjects to Post Graduate Certificate of Education (PGCE) courses, as Exhibit 23 shows. Any scheme of higher pay for scarcity subject teachers will need to include:

(a) A means of altering and, when necessary, removing altogether the pay differentials, as the shortages lessen or intensify.

(b) A means of identifying which teachers are to receive the higher payments.

(c) Information systems to show the extent of shortages and whether the shortages are due to high wastage or to recruitment difficulties.

(d) A basis for assessing the level of differential which needs to be paid.

(e) An agreed mechanism for negotiating levels of differential within the context of the rest of the negotiations of teachers' pay.

Exhibit 23

**INTAKE TO POSTGRADUATE TEACHING COURSES, 1985**

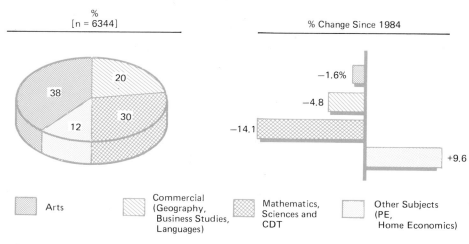

%
[n = 6344]

% Change Since 1984

−1.6%

−4.8

−14.1

+9.6

Arts

Commercial
(Geography,
Business Studies,
Languages)

Mathematics,
Sciences and
CDT

Other Subjects
(PE,
Home Economics)

Source: Audit Commission analysis of DES information on intakes to
PGCE (Secondary) course

132. In addition to differential pay, a package of measures to overcome shortages in particular subjects could include the following:

(i)   Mature specialists entering teaching from industry should enter at an appropriate incremental grade that recognises their experience; and emergency training courses should be developed for such entrants and salary paid for their duration.

(ii)  Those with qualifications in and experience of teaching scarcity subjects but who are no longer teaching should be encouraged to return, on a part-time basis if necessary.

(iii) Teaching should be promoted as a career, by steps such as active participation in the graduate recruitment "milk round".

(iv)  Staff from other disciplines with the necessary motivation and aptitude should be re-trained to teach scarcity subjects; and trainee teachers could be paid as unqualified teachers during PGCE training in scarcity subjects – this would go further than the recently announced bursary scheme.

(v)   Selected applicants for undergraduate courses could be offered bursaries throughout their degree courses, in order to compete with industrial recruitment at this stage, prior to PGCE.

(vi)  Distance teaching techniques could be developed further, for instance, using interactive video programmes.

133. However, it will be apparent that the extent of any shortage in particular subjects, the availability of possible recruits (e.g. mature specialists from industry, teachers returning to the profession, possible part-timers) and the "market" price necessary to attract them will all vary considerably from authority to authority. What is appropriate in (say) Huddersfield as an inducement to mathematics teachers would be inadequate in Newbury where computer software skills are in particular demand. Depending on the subject the market price in Newbury might, by the same token, be excessive in Penzance. So the Commission takes the view that it should be for LEAs to determine how any shortage problems should be

resolved; and they should have the flexibility within the nationally negotiated terms and conditions of service to take the necessary local action.

**Regular performance assessment**

134. In the dispute which has been running throughout the preparation of this report, assessment of teachers has been a matter of often bitter controversy. The Commission believes that every teacher's performance in adding educational 'value' to pupils should be assessed regularly and that superior performance should be reflected in relative pay levels, just as it is for instance with consultants in the National Health Service. [The Commission operates such arrangements for all its own employees]. However, the strength of the opposition to this concept runs extraordinarily deep within the education service and indeed the public service generally. Since agreement in principle by the employees to the method of assessment is an essential prerequisite to any performance-related pay arrangements, the Commission reluctantly accepts the conclusions of the Graham report* regarding merit pay that "the necessary conditions for success do not currently exist in England and Wales". In any case, the Secretary of State has removed the issue from national negotiations for the time being.

135. In the meantime, it is important that a system for consistent assessment of schools' and teachers' performance is agreed and put in place soon. Regular performance feedback is essential if individual teachers are to realise their full professional potential; training needs and promotion decisions cannot be soundly based in the absence of regular assessments. Such a system will require a clear definition of terms. In the assessment of teachers' performance it is particularly necessary to distinguish between "monitoring" which is a concern for the work, and "appraisal" which relates to the individual:

- Monitoring is about observation of job performance, operating to a defined contractual base line. For example, a contractual statement such as "the teacher will teach allocated classes and prepare and mark appropriate pupil work", would be interpreted at school level, usually by agreement, within a subject department. This may involve decisions on a particular syllabus, use of specific resources, the type and frequency of pupil written work to be set, a marking policy, etc. Once agreed, these become clearly observable elements of the teacher's work. Monitoring is the continuous process of ensuring that such a professionally agreed policy is implemented. Inspection would come within the role of the head of department and be subject to check by the head or by external advisers or inspectors. The LEA as employer has a right to expect that work paid for is being done; the teacher has a right to expect that the time and resources to do the job are available. This is the area to be covered by negotiations on conditions of service.

- Appraisal is about the judgmental or professional area, and is undertaken to improve personal performance, and therefore, perhaps, career prospects. It should seek to identify personal strengths with a view to career development and to discover weaknesses for which improvements can be sought. It should be carried out by senior staff, advisers or inspectors who would need appropriate training, and should be done at least every two years.

---

* *Those having torches . . . . teacher appraisal: a study*, Suffolk Education Department, May 1985 – ISBN 0 86055 166 0

136. The Commission considers that the details of the performance assessment arrangements and their relationship (if any) to pay should be determined by local negotiation. In particular, the extent to which the process of monitoring job performance should extend beyond the observable into areas of judgmental or professional assessment is a matter for local negotiation, as is its extension, via aptitude testing, into personal qualities. Appraisal will undoubtedly extend, if it is to be effective, into both areas, and should be beneficial to both teacher and employer, and, therefore, to pupils. If assessment of teaching is to be undertaken seriously LEAs will need to ensure that three requirements are met:

(a) Guidance: the Graham report offers much valuable assistance in the process of appraisal. Such schools and LEAs as have experience in this area are in a position to help. This is an area which is best left to local development and agreement. Monitoring of job performance could be negotiated nationally in outline and interpreted in detail within individual LEAs and schools.

(b) Information: the field work undertaken by the Commission has demonstrated current weaknesses here. None of the LEAs visited has in place a complete personnel record system for any purpose other than salary. The need for non-confidential information of a factual nature for purposes such as redeployment, early retirement or institutional planning was mentioned in Chapter One. It would also be useful for monitoring and appraisal. Within schools visited by the study team, head teachers normally had such basic information, but in by no means all cases was it regularly updated. It may be that monitoring and appraisal systems would in fact remedy this defect themselves.

(c) Resources: the implications are considerable. The Graham report refers to a total of eight to 12 hours' effort from all concerned per teacher appraised. There will also be training and development costs. Without effective resourcing any form of teacher assessment will be an impossibility.

137. Finally, in the context of teacher assessment, it will be important to avoid muddying the waters by claiming that the process will be used to "weed out" incompetent teachers. New procedures to respond to teacher incompetence are needed. These should begin with close monitoring, guidance and help for teachers seen to be failing. Should such a remedial programme fail, a dismissal procedure must be invoked which contains no suggestion of personal misconduct. In addition, the number of incompetent teachers would be reduced by a tightening up of admission to the teaching profession. At present the proportion of PGCE students to whom the certificate is not awarded is extremely low and the proportion of teachers who do not pass their probationary year is negligible. It is implausible that all those who passed were considered competent.

**Covering for absent teachers**

138. Teachers are absent from schools, or at least from the classes they normally teach, for a variety of reasons. There is also considerable variation from one part of the academic year to another in both extent and cause of such absence. These reasons include sickness, in-service training, examination administration and development, assessment needs and fieldwork. Current initiatives in education all tend to increase absence for reasons other than sickness.

139. LEAs do not usually keep records of teacher absence – their records usually deal only with sickness absence. In the course of the Special Study, the Commission conducted a survey of teacher absence in 70 schools in 12 LEAs for the autumn term of 1984. The survey showed that absence for all

reasons was 4.64 per cent of total teacher time in school – maternity leave and secondment were excluded. The figure of sickness absence (3.28) compared well with the corresponding figure for other categories of employee and with private industry. But the effect of teacher absence on the programme of work of an individual pupil is considerable, as the following illustrative calculation shows:

A school has:  830 pupils
46 teachers
4.64% absence rate
40 period week (8 per day)
0.78 contact ratio
23 average class size

On a typical day 46 x 4.64% of teachers are absent  =  2.134

Those teachers will miss the following lessons
2.134 x 0.78 x 8  =  13.32

23 x 13.32 represents the number of pupil lessons
which will therefore be missed  =  306

If, therefore, the effects of teacher absence were spread equally amongst all pupils, 37 per cent of them would lose a lesson each day or, at best, have it delivered by the wrong teacher. Moreover, the effect on other teachers is also considerable. In the illustrative example, the remaining teachers have non-contact time amounting to 43.87 x 0.22 x 8 = 77 periods. Of these, 13.32 periods or 17 per cent of non-contact time may be absorbed by the absence of other teachers.

140. As far as possible, those activities which take teachers away from the classroom should take place outside class hours. Any new conditions of service for teachers should make explicit provision for this. Part of this provision could be made by a change in the school year so that the teachers' mandatory year was longer than the pupils'. If, for instance, the teachers' year were ten days longer than the pupils', it would be possible with careful management to reduce teacher absence from classes by around 20 per cent.

141. The proportion of teacher absence covered by external supply staff is, under present conditions of service, a matter for each LEA to determine. The determination is expressed as a stated policy, for example, that absences will only be covered by a casual supply teacher after the third day; and LEA practices vary, as they probably should, given different local circumstances. Casual supply is not now normally provided through a permanent supply staff. The National Union of Teachers (NUT)found in a survey of 70 authorities that 35 had a "central pool" of supply teachers. A later shire county survey found only one with a supply pool. Figures taken from a small sample of schools in each of 12 LEAs for the autumn term 1984 show that their interpretation of LEA rules for supply allowed for anything from 14 per cent to 63 per cent of absence to be covered under the rules. The average perceived provision under LEA policy was 36 per cent.

142. The extent to which LEAs were able to deliver the level of cover implied in their policies also varied greatly. In one authority only 58 per cent of provision theoretically available under the policy could be delivered in fact; in another, the figure was 99 per cent. The average for the survey was 91 per cent. Clearly, other things being equal, it is much easier for an LEA offering cover for only 14 per cent of absence to provide what its policy stipulates. However, the most generous LEA was also able to

achieve the 91 per cent average. Difficulties in delivering the policy arise from two main sources: insufficient teachers available for casual employment in an LEA or a particular school, and inadequate systems to facilitate the tapping of such supply as exists.

143. The availability of supply teachers certainly varies widely within and between authorities. In general, it is harder for metropolitan districts to obtain supply cover than for counties, and in some areas the difficulties are extreme. Seventy per cent of the schools offering information on this referred to some difficulty in obtaining appropriate supply teachers. These ranged from schools who could easily obtain teachers but found difficulty in recruiting specialists in particular disciplines (those mentioned included mathematics, science, languages and CDT), to those which found it very difficult to recruit any supply teachers at all.

144. Support to schools in finding appropriate staff also varies greatly. Some authorities provided little assistance other than access by telephone to an officer with a list which may be months out of date. This results in the senior staff of schools spending many unnecessary hours on the telephone. Other authorities offer positive assistance of various types. The policies outlined below, all of which are followed by some authorities, are worth more general consideration:

    (a) Use of permanent supply staff in shortage subjects and in geographical areas where the general shortage is particularly acute.

    (b) Regular advertisements for supply teachers, preferably with references required and interviews of applicants.

    (c) Compilation of a list of supply teachers, checked for qualifications, qualified teacher status, and absence from list 99 (the national list of persons who have been found unsuitable to be teachers).

    (d) Regular updating of the list, where necessary by provision of reply paid envelopes, cross referencing with fixed-term and permanent appointments and regular returns from heads.

    (e) A requirement that heads should assess the success or otherwise of placements; and the provision to all schools at frequent regular intervals of a circulated list of appropriate supply teachers.

In any event, schools and teachers should at all times maintain records of schemes of classes' work so that supply teachers coming into the school are able to be clear on the work being pursued and can act as more than childminders.

145. However well external cover is managed, internal cover is likely to continue to be the main response to teacher absence. Any new conditions of service for teachers should recognise this need. One way in which the need for internal cover might be recognised is to add staff to the establishment specifically for cover purposes. All teachers would then be required to deliver a certain number of cover lessons over the course of a year. A system on this principle in one authority operates as follows:

A supply cover allowance is allocated to each school based upon the average absence level of teachers over the preceding three years. Each teacher is required to provide cover for an average of one period every two weeks, a total of 19 periods a year. The total of periods that is to be contributed by teachers is subtracted from the average absence figure and the balance added to the school's establishment.

146. The problem of using an increased school establishment to deal with cover is that of seasonality – there are peaks of absence within the school year; so the head teacher will need to manage in-service training and other programmes with appropriate care. An alternative approach, compatible with the increased delegation to schools described in Chapter One, is to include the allocation of a cash allowance for supply cover in the overall

school budget. The school will then be able to decide whether to buy in some "peak" cover as necessary, as well as determining whether greater use of part-timers or stepped down teachers would be worthwhile.

**Lunchtime supervision**

147. The Secretary of State has now accepted that the 1968 Rosetti agreement, which previously governed lunchtime supervision, is no longer operable. Funds have been made available for free standing schemes to be negotiated locally, which the Commission welcomes. The study team found that there was, before the dispute, considerable variation in the proportion of teachers ready to undertake such duties, a fact likely to be reflected in the new arrangements. They also found that, almost without exception, the secondary heads interviewed believed that ancillary staff were unable to execute such duties without substantial involvement of teaching staff. But the situation will vary among LEAs and indeed from school to school. It is clear, therefore, that arrangements must be negotiated at the local level rather than centrally.

\*      \*      \*

To sum up, the Commission believes that the next five years or so hold very great opportunities for improving secondary education, notwithstanding the present serious difficulties. But time is slipping past. And the experience of the past five years suggests the need for radical changes to the way the service is managed if the opportunity is not to be lost in a continuing welter of mutual recrimination. The final chapter of this report therefore suggests the way ahead.

# 3 Next Steps

149. It will be apparent that there is no time to lose if the opportunity presented by falling secondary school rolls is not to slip by. Perhaps as many as 1,000 schools will need to close over the next four to five years, and up to £2 billion in new capital will need to be invested in the schools that remain. As Exhibit 24 shows, these figures imply annual targets for closures and capital spending which far outstrip recent performance. Both government and LEAs have an important role to play if the next five years are to be put to good use. This chapter, therefore, summarises the key steps to be taken by each of the "players" in turn.

Exhibit 24

**SECONDARY SCHOOLS IN ENGLAND AND WALES**

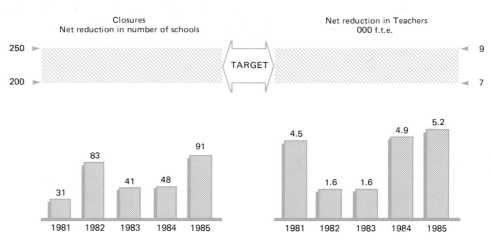

Source: CIPFA Education Statistics, 1985-86 Estimate Tables 3.1 and 3.3
Audit Commission Analysis (targets)

**RECOMMENDED ACTION BY GOVERNMENT**

150. Government has already made plain its view that secondary education needs to be improved; and it has set in train a variety of initiatives designed to improve both the quality and relevance of what is taught in secondary schools in particular. It has also made clear that it does not expect to see any additional resources made available, by the taxpayer at least. Exhibit 18 showed that capital expenditure on schools (including primary schools) in England in constant (1985) prices is planned at around £200 million. The inflation assumptions are fairly heroic; so it is reasonably safe to assume that in real terms the plans are relatively optimistic. The outturn is likely to be less favourable, particularly when set against the need to invest perhaps as much as £2 billion in secondary schools' reorganisation over the next four to five years.

151. It is not for the Commission to challenge Government policy any more than auditors may challenge LEAs' policy decisions. Nor is the Commission competent to comment on such matters as the quality of

teachers, the appropriateness of the present curriculum and streaming arrangements within schools, the way teachers' performance is best assessed, or the means of exercising parental choice; these require the expertise of educationalists, among others. The Commission's concern, and the focus of this report, is the management of secondary schools. There are several important steps in some cases involving legislation that only government can take over the next 12–18 months to help LEAs manage a very difficult local situation better:

(i) Promote new arrangements for negotiating teachers' pay and conditions of service along the lines outlined in paragraphs 113–128.

(ii) Enable and encourage more local flexibility with respect to teachers' pay and conditions of service, within a nationally agreed framework. Specifically, the Commission believes that decisions on how much needs to be paid to recruit teachers in shortage subjects, arrangements for providing cover for lunchtime supervision and ways of assessing teachers and recognising superior teaching performance should all be a local responsibility. National solutions will inevitably turn out to be sub-optimal in most local situations.

(iii) Ensure that the grant distribution arrangements and systems for controlling capital expenditure do not act as a deterrent to authorities wishing to invest in secondary school reorganisation. The Commission has already made clear its view that longer planning horizons are necessary in local government and that abrupt year-to-year changes in grant cause waste and inefficiency. In addition, paragraphs 108–112 set out some specific proposals for limiting the damage that will otherwise be done by the latest changes in the grant distribution arrangements and by the proposals for controlling local authorities' capital spending.

(iv) Limit the involvement of the Secretary of State in reviewing school reorganisation plans to the most controversial proposals; this would be possible if there was an order-of-magnitude increase in the number of formal objections required for a scheme to be "called in" by the Secretary of State. At present objections from ten local electors will suffice; this is an absurdly small number.

(v) Provide more incentives to local communities to accept initially unpalatable reorganisation proposals; and strengthen local accountability by ensuring that some of the additional costs incurred as a result of delay to a scheme agreed by the relevant LEA fall as a charge on those responsible for the hold-up. The mechanics of such a scheme are not immediately obvious. However, it is evident that some way must be found of forcing protesters to consider both sides of the value for money equation if reorganisation is to move ahead on the scale and at the pace required. At present, protesters are able to impose what are in effect additional taxes on their fellow citizens absolutely free, and without any need to consult those who are paying for the cost of the protest.

(vi) Provide for LEAs to have the same powers with respect to voluntary aided schools as they do with other secondary schools over redeploying teachers, except in the case of teachers of religious education.

(vii) Empower LEAs to offer voluntary severance to teachers.

**LEAS' RESPONSIBILITIES**

152. Since this report is mainly about the way teachers are managed and since teachers are employed by LEAs it follows that the authorities have the major part of the responsibility for taking action on the recommendations set out in the previous two chapters. Specifically, this report has suggested

that all authorities should take the following steps as a matter of urgency:

(i) Re-examine their strategies with respect to school closures: are plans agreed to protect and preferably enhance the curriculum at costs which the local ratepayers would be willing to pay? Unless substantial rate rises are deemed to be acceptable, a number of schools should already be programmed for closure. Obviously the precise scale of the reorganisation required will depend on the local circumstances; but the following is a guide for LEAs facing different falls in rolls but with a typical size distribution in their schools.

*Table 18:* SCALE OF SCHOOL CLOSURES TO BE EXAMINED
% Current schools – illustrative

| Projected fall in rolls (1981 – 1991) | Population density | | |
|---|---|---|---|
| | High | Medium | Low |
| ≤10% | 10% | 5 | – |
| 11 – 20 | 15 | 10 | 5 |
| 21 – 30 | 25 | 20 | 15 |
| 31 – 40 | 30 | 25 | 20 |

(ii) Ensure that every school's complement of teachers is compatible with a level of curricular provision agreed by the authority. This implies that, as a first step, all LEAs should agree a curriculum model with head teachers and governing bodies. The ALS approach described in the Appendix will allow overall staffing to be related to the curriculum in each school. Where the curriculum model indicates a need for more teachers than the authority is willing to afford, local decisions must be made on either:
   – adjustments in curricular provision;
   – relaxation of the group size constraints for particular subjects and year groups, or
   – changes in the allocation of teacher time for non-classroom duties, or
   – changes in the structure of the local secondary school system.

(iii) Improve local manpower planning for teachers, with a view to minimising the need for early retirement or voluntary redundancies in the near term and avoiding unduly heavy recruitment programmes in the early 1990s: the first is needlessly expensive and disruptive of sound labour relations; the latter will almost certainly lead to a fall in quality of new entrants to the profession. This implies that every LEA should have:
   – detailed projections of teacher strength at each school;
   – LEA-wide gap analysis, identifying gross over- and under-staffing by schools and subject specialism;
   – analysis of the training needs of the existing teacher force, enabling targeted in-service training programmes to fill vacancies in shortage subjects in particular;
   – more redeployment of teachers from one school to another;
   – more use of part-time teachers;
   – limited use of ring fences, particularly when advertising for heads and their deputies and for teachers in shortage subjects.
   Exhibit 25 (overleaf) summarises a possible timing of the annual process within an LEA for filling staff vacancies.

(iv) Delegate as much responsibility as possible to heads and governing bodies, together with the authority necessary to discharge it. Any increase in delegated managerial responsibility to the school level must be contingent upon:

75

Exhibit 25

**POSSIBLE TIMETABLE FOR FILLING STAFF VACANCIES**

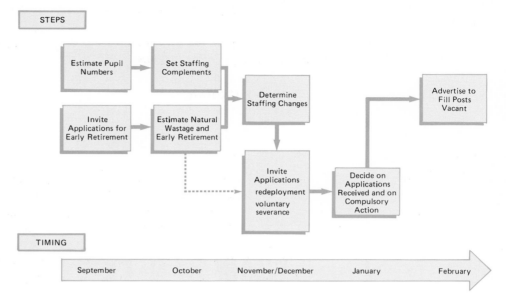

– Sound planning and control procedures so that the LEA is not abdicating, as opposed to delegating, its statutory responsibilities;

– LEAs and governors paying greater attention to the selection of head teachers, adopting a more professional and planned approach;

– More management training for all candidates wishing to be considered for appointment as deputy heads and heads.

(v) Develop local strategies for recruiting teachers for shortage subjects, managing teacher absence, providing cover for lunchtime supervision and recognising superior teaching performance. As stated above, the Commission considers that, present arrangements notwithstanding, each of these problems is more appropriately tackled locally – in some cases at the school rather than the LEA level. However, some careful planning and policy guidance from the authority will obviously be required. Since there is likely to be little notice of any change to the present arrangements, LEAs will be well advised to undertake the preparatory staff work now – this might even be useful in informing DES decisions.

(vi) Jointly enter into negotiations with teachers' associations to establish a teachers' year which is longer than the pupils. This will make joint teacher activities – including, particularly, in-service training – more possible without harmful effects on pupil contact.

\*     \*     \*

The Commision's auditors will be working with authorities in the coming 18 months to help ensure that the appropriate local action is in hand. Every LEA will receive a report on the extent to which the local education service is taking full advantage of the opportunities that falling rolls may present to improve secondary education – to the benefit of pupils, teachers and those who pay for the service and ultimately the nation's economic performance and social cohesion. In the Commission's view, it would be nothing short of tragic if this one-off opportunity is lost through managerial incompetence or lack of will locally or at the national level.

# Appendix

## ILLUSTRATIONS OF ACTIVITY-LED STAFFING

1. This appendix describes in turn the application of the Activity-Led Staffing (ALS) approach to:
   (a) A lower school
   (b) A sixth form
   (c) Non-classroom activities

**STAFFING FOR THE MAIN SCHOOL**

2. The number of periods of the week for which each subject is to be taught and the sizes of pupil groups for different subjects are specified. These two factors determine the number of teacher periods that are required. So, if there are 180 pupils and the maximum group size is 25, say for science, then 8 groups will be needed. If the particular subject for which this group size applies is taught for 2 periods a week the number of periods for which a teacher is required for this group, the number of teacher periods in the timetable, is equal to 2 (periods) multiplied by 8 (groups), a total of 16.

3. This process can be repeated for all subjects and year groups. Similarly, a year group of 220 pupils, organised in groups with a maximum size of 30 for 5 periods of the week, say for English, would require 8 groups and 40 teacher periods.

4. The process is illustrated in Table A–1, which shows the calculation of staffing for a first-year group.

*Table A–1:* CURRICULUM STAFFING FOR A GROUP OF FIRST YEAR PUPILS

Size of Pupil Group = 180

| Subject (a) | Periods per week (b) | Group size (max.) (c) | No. of groups (d) | Teacher periods (b x d) |
|---|---|---|---|---|
| English | 5 | 30 | 6 | 30 |
| Mathematics | 5 | 30 | 6 | 30 |
| Humanities (Hist, Geog, RE) | 7 | 30 | 6 | 42 |
| Language* (French & German) | 8 | 30 | 3 | 24 |
| Language** (French only) | 5 | 30 | 3 | 15 |
| Science | 6 | 25 | 8 | 48 |
| Music | 1 | 30 | 6 | 6 |
| Art | 2 | 20 | 9 | 18 |
| Crafts* | 3 | 20 | 5 | 15 |
| Crafts** | 6 | 20 | 5 | 30 |
| PE | 3 | 30 | 6 | 18 |

| | |
|---|---|
| Total teacher periods | 276 |
| Periods per week in timetable | 40 |
| Staff required for classroom teaching duties [276 ÷ 40] | 6.9 |

\*   1/2 year group have French 5 and Crafts 6
\*\*  1/2 year group have French 5, German 3 and Crafts 3

There might also be additions for special needs such as remedial provision.

5. The curriculum is more varied in the fourth and fifth years because pupils are normally free to choose courses from a range of possible options. The process of calculating the number of teacher periods required is largely the same, as shown in Table A–2. In the fourth and fifth year each option would be chosen from a "block" of options containing a number of subject

77

choices, say six. The more of the curriculum is dealt with in the core, the fewer the number of option blocks. Models also make additions for particular needs, such as the need for remedial work, or for boys and girls to be taught PE in separate groups.

*Table A–2:* CURRICULUM STAFFING FOR FOURTH OR FIFTH YEAR
Size of pupil group = 180

| Subject (a) | Periods per week (b) | Group size (max.) (c) | No. of groups (d) | Teacher periods (b x d) |
|---|---|---|---|---|
| English | 6 | 25 | 8 | 48 |
| Mathematics | 5 | 25 | 8 | 40 |
| RE | 1 | 25 | 8 | 8 |
| PE | 3 | 25 | 8 | 24 |
| Careers | 1 | 25 | 8 | 8 |
| Option 1 | 4 | 20 | 9 | 36 |
| Option 2 | 4 | 20 | 9 | 36 |
| Option 3 | 4 | 20 | 9 | 36 |
| Option 4 | 4 | 20 | 9 | 36 |
| Option 5 | 4 | 20 | 9 | 36 |
| Option 6 | 4 | 20 | 9 | 36 |
| | | | | 344 |
| Staff required for classroom duties [344 ÷ 40] | | | | 8.6 |

Both examples are given to illustrate part of the process of activity-led staffing. They are not expressions of an Audit Commission view of an appropriate level of provision.

**STAFFING FOR SIXTH FORMS**

6. The ALS model for a sixth form of 100 could be as follows:

| | Teacher periods |
|---|---|
| General studies (including PE & RE), lower sixth and upper sixth taught jointly for 8 periods in groups of 20 | 40 |
| 14 A level subjects, involving 8 periods each, of which 10 A levels taught separately to lower and upper sixth | 160 |
| 4 A levels taught jointly for 50 per cent of time, and separately for 50 per cent of time, | 48 |
| 10 Non-A level sets for 4 periods | 40 |
| Total teacher periods required | 288 |
| Staff required for classroom duties | 7.2 |

7. In practice things are likely to be much more complex than in this simple example. As post-16 education expands and becomes more varied, pupils can pursue a very wide range of courses – O levels, A levels, BTEC, CGLI, CSE, CPVE and many others. Not all courses demand the same number of periods per week or number of years of study and the relative popularity of subjects may change from year to year and school to school. Pupils may not be taught for the whole of the week, but use time for private study. Students may be studying part-time rather than full-time. A further major difficulty is knowing how many will actually turn up in the sixth form at the beginning of the year. In the study authorities many predictions of sixth form numbers were found to be inaccurate.

8. These need to be identified and given weightings which may differ between LEAs or even between schools. Such duties can be divided, into four groups:

- Those functions relating to each school and which will not vary greatly with the size of school.
- Those functions relating to individual teachers.
- Those functions relating to individual pupils.
- Other classes of activity.

Table A–3 shows a sample build-up allowing for activities in the first three groups.

*Table A–3:* SAMPLE ACTIVITY LIST

| | Days/Year |
|---|---|
| **School-related activities** | |
| Policy decision making | |
| Finance and resource assessment | |
| Monitoring of senior staff policy making and action | |
| LEA and government returns | |
| External relations: LEA, media, community, etc. | |
| Examination administration; liaison with boards | |
| Preparation of prospectuses, governors' reports, etc. | |
| | 200 |
| | |
| **Teacher-related activities** | |
| Substitution for absent staff | 5 |
| Appointment of staff | 0.5 |
| Communication and consultation processes | 0.5 |
| Curriculum planning and development | 1 |
| Timetable creation and maintenance | 1 |
| Stock ordering and control | 0.5 |
| Staff management (monitoring and present informal appraisal) | 1 |
| Clerical and other routine tasks | 3 |
| Supervision of ancillary staff | 0.5 |
| Lesson preparation | 12 |
| In-service training and induction of new teachers | 5 |
| Total | 30 |

[The requirements here are expressed in terms of days per 100 per cent teaching timetable. Requirements cannot logically be stated in terms of the full number of teachers to be employed since this list of activities is being drawn up to determine that requirement.]

| | |
|---|---|
| **Pupil-related activities** | |
| Support for fieldwork and residential studies | 0.5 |
| Liaison with parents | 2.0 |
| Record keeping (marks, profiles, letters) | 0.75 |
| Reports and references | 1.25 |
| Pastoral and disciplinary work | 1 |
| Educational and vocational guidance | 0.5 |
| Application of options structures | 0.25 |
| Marking and individual follow-up work | 2 |
| Total | 8.25 |

9. On the assumption that the time allocation relates only to those elements of a teacher's work which should be fitted into the school day, assume that:

| the teacher day | = | 6 hours |
|---|---|---|
| 1 teacher day per year | = | 0.005 of a full time teacher |

If the values in the table above were adopted, the requirement for staffing beyond classroom work would be calculated thus:

school tasks     = 1

teacher tasks    = X x 0.15     (where X is the staffing establishment calculated according to the curriculum model without contact ratio applied)

pupil tasks      = Y x 0.005    (where Y is the total number of pupils)

10. The following table shows examples of the results of the above process in different types of school using only the three basic functions of school, teacher and pupil related activities. It is, of course, variable according to the needs of individual LEAs.

*Table A–4:* FOUR ILLUSTRATIVE EXAMPLES
Total teacher staffing

|  | | Schools | | | |
| --- | --- | --- | --- | --- | --- |
|  | | A | B | C | D |
|  | Age group | 11–18 | 11–18 | 12–16 | 6th form |
|  | Pupils | 718 | 1587 | 1063 | 395 |
| Staffing to teach curriculum model | | 34.30 | 69.60 | 44.70 | 22.90 |
| School activities | | 1.00 | 1.00 | 1.00 | 1.00 |
| Staff activities | | 5.15 | 10.44 | 6.70 | 3.44 |
| Pupil activities | | 3.60 | 7.94 | 5.32 | 1.98 |
| TOTAL STAFFING | | 44.05 | 88.98 | 57.72 | 29.32 |
| [Equivalent contact ratio | | 0.78 | 0.78 | 0.77 | 0.78] |

Printed in the UK for HMSO Dd239974 C10. 9/86 49818